School Dinners

School Dinners

Becky Thorn

PORTICO

First published in the United Kingdom in 2008 by
Portico Books
10 Southcombe Street
London
W14 0RA

An imprint of Anova Books Company Ltd

This book can be ordered direct from the publisher.
Contact the marketing department, but try your bookshop first.

ISBN: 9781906032449

A CIP catalogue record for this book is available from the British Library.

Design Manager: Gemma Wilson
Designer: Matt Windsor and Abby Franklin
Illustrator: Matt Windsor

10 9 8 7 6 5 4 3 2 1

Reproduction by Rival Colour Ltd, UK
Printed and bound by WS Bookwell, Finland

www.anovabooks.com

Contents

*Thank you to M, Z and C for indulging
my obsession and for asking for seconds
when I finally got a recipe right.*

*Dinnerladies and school cooks the country over,
I raise my scoop in salute.*

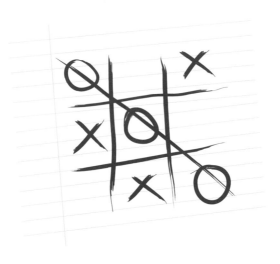

Introduction

Did you lust after a chopper or crack your knuckles on clackers? Did you cut the roof of your mouth on Spangles or fancy the Milky Bar Kid? If you did, then like me, you lived through the heyday of school dinners – a time when all schools had a cook, each cook had her ice-cream scoop and she wasn't afraid to use it!

My own school-meal memories didn't start too well. Clean plates were the order of the day and if you had asked for an item to be put on your plate it was assumed you wanted it and would eat it. As a new four-year-old member of the school I didn't know this and when baked beans appeared on my plate I thought I could leave them as the texture made me gag. I tried to explain this to the dinner lady but she was having none of it. She tried persuasion, bribery and then just decided to spoon the beans in. Bad move really as they bounced along with the rest of my meal, all over her legs and feet. Needless to say she never made me eat beans again.

Even with this less than glorious beginning I went on to relish school meals. My school-meal eating years were between 1968 and 1983 as a pupil and from 1987 until the present day as a teacher. My children cannot believe you had to eat liver and bacon at school, and my husband can't believe I had seconds. But I did because that got me at the front of the queue for puddings, somewhere you will still find me today. Some were real traditional favourites such as jam tart whilst others, like chocolate concrete, were only found in school canteens. Pies and casseroles, both filling and nutritious, were the order of the day, Occasionally a curry or spaghetti Bolognaise would ring a more exotic note. Roast dinners with all the trimmings made our week complete. Gravies, sauces and custards washed down the trickier mouthfuls and treats such as cornflake tart, chocolate sponge and chocolate custard set our hearts racing.

I have a very precious book filled with handwritten recipes that belonged to my Mum. I use it all the time, cooking recipes written down by family members that bring back long-distant memories as the familiar smells fill the kitchen. Being a creature of habit I tend to cook the dishes I remember best, but I also love to read through the recipes as a form of gastroporn.

One summer's day, I found myself flicking through, wondering what else might be lurking in this book. There were fabulous time-warp recipes from the early part of my Mum's married life, Blue Peter recipes written in my brother's and sister's very young handwriting, and some very ambitious recipes cut from colour supplements and glued in place. Then, folded neatly and tucked in between the pages of the book, was a very tatty piece of paper. Opening the paper I saw it was the back of a school newsletter from my infant school. After requests for dressing-up clothes and a reminder that school finished on 21 December for the Christmas holidays came the following lines:

Butterscotch tart

6oz margarine
6oz brown sugar
$1^{1}/_{2}$ oz flour
$3^{1}/_{2}$ oz milk

Line a tin with pastry and bake. Melt margarine and milk, and boil – add sugar and flour – cook – allow to cool – spread on pastry.

Thank you Mrs Ash and the canteen staff for giving us this lovely recipe.

Butterscotch tart I remembered from school vividly. It was my favourite pudding but not one I can ever recall my mum cooking for us. I had to try it out and see if it was as I recalled. It was better, dense and chewy with just a hint of toothache. The custard melted the toffee topping just as I hoped too. More to the point, my children loved it as much as me.

The butterscotch tart recipe set me thinking: what other lovely school dinners could I re-create to share with my family? I sat down and wrote a list of all the meals I had had at school. I knew somewhere I had several recipes from my days as a teacher that I had persuaded a school cook to let me have. These became the basis of my school dinners' recipe collection. I asked friends when I saw them what meals they enjoyed, I asked people I barely knew at my sister's 40th birthday party what they remembered and liked best.

I was, I fear, a little obsessed. Every meal I cooked was a school-dinner variation. Given it was the height of summer and I was making suet pastry for tea, my family began to rebel. I even managed to get on to local radio to discuss my 'guilty pleasure' and persuaded the host to try some of the recipes I had by then re-created live on air. Eating on the radio can be a tricky business. What had started as a way to record my favourite recipes for my children just as my mum had done for me, grew and grew until we have the eighty recipes you see here in this book.

School dinners had a real quirkiness about them I discovered. If a dish was labelled a pie then it had a topping of some form, be it pastry, suet or potato. It did not, however, have a bottom. Tarts had bottoms but they never had tops and they were almost always sweet, which brought a smile to many an adolescent in the seventies. A savoury tart was known as a flan, as the word quiche was something only Margot would say in *The Good Life*. Food almost always had corners, served from large rectangular aluminium tins. Meals you expected to have curves, like steak and kidney pudding, suddenly became much more linear, and surely schools are the only places where jelly was served cut into cuboids. Many have accused school meals of being beige and brown, but having created these recipes I think this is unfair. Yes, there was a lot of gravy and custard, but there was quite a lot of food colouring too and who can forget the vibrancy of a ruby-red tinned tomato nestled up against a slice of bright-yellow cheese flan?

***

School dinners have come a long way since they were first conceived. In the very earliest days they were seen as a way to prevent the poorest of children from slipping further into a nutritional crisis. The provision varied from authority to authority and only helped those with the greatest need. The advent of war and the movement of so many evacuated children around the country caused the government to think again about school-meal provision. It was the 1944 Education Act that made it a statutory duty of local authorities to provide a heavily subsidised school-meals service and gave us free school milk. The Act even stipulated that the meal of two courses should provide 42% of the daily protein and at least 33% of the overall energy requirement.

By the 1970s, the school dinner heyday, 70% of children had a school meal. But then came the 1980 Education Act. Margaret Thatcher, who as Education Minister in the early 1970s had already been labelled 'milk snatcher' for stopping free school milk for all, returned to bang the final nail in the coffin of school meals as we remember them.

Local authorities no longer had to provide a school-meals service and the nutritional standards were removed from the Act. Instead, authorities were allowed to put the service out to tender and the numbers of children eating school meals spiralled down more rapidly than a droplet of fat oozing its way out from a turkey twizzler. The very small amounts of money set aside for each meal now meant a reliance on cheap mass-produced food often of low nutritional value and high fat content.

Since Jamie Oliver exposed this serious issue, things have begun to swing back towards home cooked meals, real meat and proper puddings at last. The calorie content has come down and choice has increased, and there seem to be more children having school dinners.

Lifestyles have changed since the sixties and seventies, and we cannot return to children having the same sorts of school meals that we loved. Britain is a very different place – vegetarianism is understood now for a start! Lives were slower, winters were colder and non-league Wimbledon

FC got to play Leeds in the FA Cup. School meals were the main meal of the day. When you got home you had your tea but you certainly didn't get another large cooked meal. This varied from home to home. If your mum was in you might get scrambled eggs or cheese on toast, a slice of cake and some squash. If your mum worked then you made yourself a jam sandwich and searched at the back of the cupboard for a chocolate tea cake or a Wagon Wheel. Lots of time was spent outside playing either on the street or in the park. The filling meals and high-calorie puddings were made for a reason. We needed the energy to play.

We walked to and from school. Families had only one car if they had one at all and it wasn't going to be used for a journey you could walk. The oil crisis and petrol rationing loomed large in all our lives and the lack of traffic meant crossing roads was not as dangerous as it is perceived to be today.

School cooks had to get large quantities of food out to the hungry masses. Time constraints meant that preparation time was of the essence and meals were made with the minimum number of ingredients. The food was tasty and nutritious, filling and fun. It is what I, as a working mum, want for my family now. I won't be feeding them high-calorie puddings every day but occasionally they are fine and if they love them as much as I do then writing them down will have all been worthwhile. Dinner ladies of the world, I salute you!

***

In this book I hope you will find tastes that awaken memories of your days at school. Food is a fantastic way to time travel. Transport yourself back to a time when tank tops were cool and lapels were so wide they could catch on doorframes. Take a few friends with you whilst you are about it. All you really need is a tray of mashed potato and an ice-cream scoop and off you go.

School pies were fantastic. Tasty toppings were cut through carefully and gave way to the slowly cooked fillings hiding underneath. Pies – sometimes crunchy, occasionally stodgy, but always delicious.

Experienced hands made the pastry and for the most part took pride in their work. These pastry-topped pies included chicken, steak and minced meat pies. Pastry wrapped around sausage meat gave us the sausage plait. Suet-topped steak and kidney pudding was a warming winter favourite. Soft and seriously comforting, the cottage pie raised our spirits after a spelling test. Fish pie was sophisticated and fulfilled any religious obligation we may have had. If we were not religious then the smell of it cooking let us all know that the weekend was on its way. Cobblers on the menu had us giggling and smirking as only teenagers can.

These were pies designed for children who walked to school, played outside and whose televisions were in black and white.

The pie recipes in this section reflect the simplicity needed when catering for 150 children. Life was too hectic to over-complicate dishes. The pies had to be simple to execute, appealing to children and value for money. Food left or thrown away was money wasted. Suggestions have been added if you want to make the pie more sophisticated or elaborate.

Make the simple version first though and serve with cabbage, mash and gravy. I guarantee you will be searching the TV guide for reruns of The Tomorrow People before you get to the puddings. Ah, the puddings ... but that is another section and a whole other story.

* * *

Each recipe makes sufficient for a family of four with some left over for seconds.

Pies

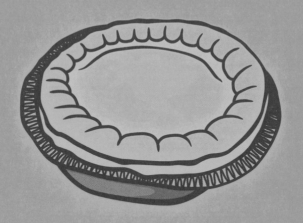

Beef pie or cobbler

In the days before heated floors, global warming or even effective radiators your parents were obsessed with keeping you warm. Tuck your vest in; don't get a chill on your kidneys. Too right – a chilled kidney was an over-productive one and sitting in an unheated school toilet was not a good place to be.

Not content with just their kidneys, boys' heads were kept warm with balaclavas, lovingly knitted by grannies and therefore ill-fitting and itchy. Taking one off came with the prospect of being caught by a teacher and being told to put it back on. You couldn't lose it either – the carefully sewn-in name tape ensured it boomeranged back to you however far you kicked it under the shoe racks in the cloakroom.

Girls couldn't escape being wrapped up either. Matching hats and scarves with tassels and pompoms adorned the coat pegs daily. The owner of a jacket made from crochet squares was always the talk of the playground.

In the cold winters beef pie or cobbler worked like a hot-water bottle for your intestines. Really this is just a beef casserole with a stodgy top. The pastry was always crispy on top with a slightly soggy gravy-infused bottom. Cobblers (insert own schoolboy snigger here!) were always cheesy and rang the changes by being round. In a world where everything came out of rectangular tins this was, excuse the pun, revolutionary.

Ingredients

500g stewing steak
1 onion, finely chopped
3 carrots, chopped
½ pint water or stock
2 tbsp flour
Pepper and salt
Herbs
Oil
Beaten egg to glaze
Shortcrust pastry or cobbler topping

How to...

1. Cut steak into cubes. Place flour into a bowl and season well with the salt and pepper. A school cook may have added dried mixed herbs too if she felt she could get away with it. Toss the meat in the flour and coat well. Leave to one side for a few minutes.

2. Heat 2tbsp of oil in a large pan and add the floured beef. Cook until the beef is well browned and then add the onion. Continue to cook out until the onion has softened but not taken on any colour.

3. Add the stock or water and cover the beef, then bring to barely simmering point. Reduce the heat right down, cover and leave for 2 hours, stirring occasionally.

4. After 2 hours, check the seasoning and add the carrots. Cover again and leave for a further 30 minutes.

5. Meanwhile heat the oven to 200°C/Gas 6 and make either the shortcrust pastry or cobbler topping (see recipes in Extras section).

6. Place the cooked beef mixture into a baking dish and top with cobbler rounds or cover with pastry.

7. Brush the topping with beaten egg and bake for 25 to 30 minutes until golden brown.

8. Serve with mashed potatoes, green vegetables and extra gravy.

Chicken pie

The school wall was often used by adults in the playground as a gaoler. A miscreant or irritating child would be told to 'stand by the wall for five minutes'. All very well and good you might think: five minutes time out, but dinner ladies were busy and often forgetful. If someone fell over, wet themselves or just got the dinner lady chatting she might not come and get you for a good half an hour.

If you complained about this forgetfulness the least you would get was a sharp reminder that if you'd been good in the first place you wouldn't have been there. Dinner ladies didn't do 'Sorry' when I was little. If they took offence at your cheekiness and they had had a really cold and taxing playtime you might get 'forgotten' again until the whistle blew.

What a dilemma chicken pies used to cause me. Was I in a pastry-eating mood or a chicken-eating one? Which part did I eat first and which was saved for later? Can I manage to manipulate my place in the queue without being spotted by a dinner lady? Why would I risk life and limb – as I said, those dinner ladies were scary – for an edge piece? Try this recipe and find out.

🖊 Ingredients

500g cooked chicken

1 onion, finely chopped

3 carrots, chopped

$\frac{1}{2}$ pint water plus a cup of chicken stock

25g flour

50g butter

Pepper and salt

Fresh tarragon or parsley

Lemon juice

Milk or beaten egg to glaze

Shortcrust pastry

How to...

① Preheat the oven to 200°C/Gas 6.

② Cut the chicken into cubes. If you don't have cooked chicken you could use 500g of chicken, breasts and thighs, taken off the bone and cooked before making up this pie.

③ Melt half the butter in a large pan and add the onion. Sweat the onion for 10 minutes until soft but not coloured. Add the carrots and toss in the butter and onion mixture. Pour in a cup of stock and simmer gently until the stock has reduced to almost nothing. Place the onion and carrots into the bottom of a, yes you guessed it, rectangular pie dish or casserole dish.

④ Melt the remaining butter in a saucepan and stir in the flour. Keep stirring until the floury flavour has been cooked out. This will take a few minutes but no longer than 5. Gradually pour in the stock, stirring constantly to prevent lumps (I know this is school dinners cooking but some things are a little too authentic). When all the stock is combined simmer gently for another 5 minutes.

⑤ Season your sauce with a good pinch of salt and freshly ground black pepper. Taste to check seasoning. A squeeze of lemon juice and a handful of chopped tarragon wouldn't go amiss either.

⑥ Place the chicken into the pie dish and pour over the sauce. Give it a stir to combine the flavours.

⑦ Top the pie with a shortcrust pastry (see recipe in Extras). Brush with a milk or egg wash. Bake for 25 to 30 minutes or until the pie crust is golden brown.

✳ Variations

If you want to make this pie a little more special you could use some wine instead of just stock when making the sauce. This is a velouté sauce and the addition of double cream just before the simmering stage also makes it much richer. Add what you want – if you have mushrooms then add them. It will give the children something to pick out too!

Minced-meat pie

Not the Christmas mincemeat pies, I'm afraid. The pie I am talking about here was the brown and beige pastry-topped savoury pie. No cream or brandy butter here, sadly, but this one came with extra gravy if you smiled sweetly at the dinner lady.

Minced-meat pie at our school was served with boiled potatoes and at least one other vegetable. The mince in our pies was fairly indeterminate leading to the usual playground rumours of stewed squirrel or minced kangaroo being the main component of the dish. I didn't care, covered in plenty of gravy pies taste great. I am almost certain the filling was beef or lamb.

Despite the vegetables in this pie it was very popular. The secret of minced-meat pie was the long slow cooking of the mince. This also had the added benefit of making the vegetables cook down to mush so we were not aware of their existence. School cooks were very savvy and they knew that if they left any part of a carrot or celery stick visible to the naked eye the offending vegetables would have been picked out and left on the edge of the plate. Children knew what was good for them and avoided it like the plague. Parents, I think you will find this is still true today.

✐ Ingredients

500g lean minced beef (if you want to try and source
minced squirrel or kangaroo, be my guest)

2 tbsp oil

1 onion, finely chopped

3 carrots, chopped

3 sticks of celery, chopped

½ pint beef stock

2 tsp Marmite

Pepper and salt

1 tsp dried mixed herbs or 1 tbsp fresh herbs

Milk or beaten egg to glaze

Shortcrust pastry

How to...

1. Preheat the oven to 200°C/Gas 6.

2. Heat half the oil in a pan and add the onion, carrots and celery. Stir to coat and cook gently until softened but not coloured. Remove to a bowl and cover.

3. Heat the remaining oil in the pan if needed and add the minced beef. Cook the meat until browned. Keep the mince moving and break up any large lumps of meat with your wooden spoon. School cooks sometimes missed this bit out and these lumps may have led in part to the squirrel-pie rumours.

4. Don't worry if the meat appears to catch a little on the base of the pan. These brown sticky bits add flavour. However, large black patches are burnt bits and are not to be encouraged!

5. Return the onion, carrot and celery to the meat and stir again. Add the Marmite to the stock and add to the meat in the pan. Stir to loosen the stickiness on the bottom of the pan. If you are using dried herbs add them now.

6. Bring up to a simmer and then reduce the heat until the surface of the meat barely moves. Cover and leave for at least an hour and a half, stirring occasionally.

7. After about an hour and a half the stock should have reduced to thickish gravy and the meat should be very tender. If the gravy isn't as thick as you want it raise the temperature and reduce the sauce down further. Check for seasoning and add fresh herbs now.

8. Pour the meat into a baking dish. Cover with a shortcrust pastry lid (see recipe in Extras) and give an egg or milk wash. Bake for 25 to 30 minutes or until golden brown.

9. Serve with boiled potatoes, peas or beans and lashings of gravy.

✳ Variations

If you want to make this pie a little more special you could use some red wine instead of just stock.

Cottage pie

Children at school were always losing teeth. Fortunately the majority of these losses were caused by the natural aging process. Sometimes there were rumours of a swift upper cut actually connecting in a playground fight, but this was a rare occurrence.

For some reason known only to the human body, once one tooth drops out several others swiftly follow. The pastry that came with either one or both school-dinner courses would often help a wobbly tooth on its way. Placed under the pillow this was a surefire way to gain a few pennies for the piggy bank without having to kiss the cheek of a bristly maiden aunt.

However, the same pastry posed a real problem for the seriously gappy child. It needed a fair amount of chewing before it could be swallowed, especially if you got an edge piece. Seeing cottage pie on the menu kept a rather spacious smile on a toothless child's face.

The uninitiated might expect this to be the same as the minced-meat pie with a mashed potato topping. Oh no, cottage pie is a different beast altogether. For some reason peas always found their way into the pie filling along with tomatoes. An ice-cream scoop was often used to spoon the mash onto the top, giving the finished dish the look of a lumpy eiderdown.

✎ Ingredients

500g lean minced beef

2 tbsp oil

1 onion, finely chopped

1 cup frozen peas

1 tin of chopped tomatoes

$\frac{1}{2}$ pint beef stock

1 kg mashing potatoes

Butter

Milk

Pepper and salt

How to...

1. Preheat the oven to 200°C/Gas 6.

2. Heat half the oil in a pan and add the onion. Stir to coat and cook gently until softened but not coloured. Remove to a bowl and cover.

3. Heat the remaining oil in the pan if needed and add the minced beef. Cook the beef until browned. Keep the mince moving and break up any large lumps of meat with your wooden spoon.

4. Return the onion to the meat and stir again. Add the tomatoes and peas to the meat in the pan. Slosh in the stock to cover the meat and vegetables. Stir to loosen the stickiness on the bottom of the pan.

5. Bring up to a simmer and then reduce the heat until the surface of the meat just shivers. Cover and leave for at least an hour and a half, stirring occasionally.

6. With about 20 minutes to go put the potatoes on to boil. Cutting the potatoes up small will help speed up the cooking process. When cooked through drain well and leave in the colander over the warm pan to dry out a little.

7. If you have a potato ricer please use as it virtually guarantees lump-free mash. If you don't have one, put it on your birthday list and get a child or a guest to mash the potato for you. Doing this gives you time to have a quick mouthful of wine and prevents them from complaining that the mash is lumpy as they made it! Stir in butter and milk to taste.

8. After about an hour and a half the stock should have reduced to thickish gravy and the mince should be very tender. If the gravy isn't as thick as you want it raise the temperature and reduce the sauce down further. Check seasoning.

9. Pour the meat into a baking dish and top with the potatoes. Bake for 25 minutes or until the topping is golden and bubbly.

✳ Variations

If you want to make this pie a little more special you could use some red wine instead of just stock.

Fish pie

One year Friday was our swimming day. Every week we'd troop out to the coach and wait, clutching our bags, to be counted on to the coach. Both classes went at the same time and by some miracle we managed to squeeze onto the one coach.

Once changed and with our clothes in a locker we would line up facing the wall to have our feet checked. 'Don't let me have a verruca,' you thought. Hats were pulled on and the straps done up under the chin. The unluckier girls had the flowery hats they had borrowed from their mums. Long-haired boys regretted being fashionable as soon as the swimming teacher lent them the school swimming cap.

One good thing was that swimming made you hungry and even though I didn't like fish that much I always finished my fish pie.

The pie I remember was made using only white fish fillets and I am sure it wasn't cod. For an island nation fish once a week seems very limiting, but this recipe was rich and tasty even if it appeared pale and uninteresting. The cook sometimes made it look more exciting by adding a layer of spinach to the pie. This made the fish pie look better and it gave us something to pick out!

Ingredients

500g coley or haddock

1 pint milk

1 kg mashing potatoes, peeled and cubed

1 bag spinach

1 tbsp butter

2 tbsp plain flour

Pepper and salt

Bay leaf

Nutmeg

Peppercorns

How to...

1. Preheat the oven to 200°C/Gas 6.
2. Place the fish in a shallow saucepan and cover with the milk. Add a bay leaf and a few peppercorns. Bring slowly to the boil and then remove from the heat and rest for 5 minutes or so. Lift the fish on to a plate and strain and reserve the cooking liquor. Discard the peppercorns and bay leaf.
3. Wash the spinach and place in a hot pan with no additional water. Cook down, stirring all the time. When fully wilted place in a sieve to drain. Layer the drained spinach into the bottom of a rectangular casserole or pie dish. Grate a little nutmeg over the spinach if you wish.
4. Put the potatoes on to boil before you make the sauce.
5. Melt the butter gently in a saucepan and gradually add the flour little by little until the butter is all used up. This may not use all the flour. Cook the butter and flour mixture (roux) for a few minutes. Reduce the heat under the roux and then slowly add the reserved cooking liquor little by little, stirring all the time. Carry on adding the milk until the sauce has the consistency of thick cream.
6. Flake the fish into the sauce, removing any stray bones as you go and pour this saucy mixture over the spinach.
7. Mash your potatoes with a little butter and milk and, using a spatula, smooth over the fish mixture. Rough up the surface of the fish pie with a fork. No ice-cream scoops here. It was one way of telling if it was fish or shepherd's pie, if the smell didn't give it away that is.
8. Bake for 25 minutes or until the pie is golden.

✳ *Variations*

If you want to make this pie a little more special you could use some salmon fillets or a few prawns to make a more varied filling. I'm not a great fan of the fish–cheese combination but if you are, then making a cheesy mash topping might just float your boat!

Cheese flan

Wednesday was my favourite day at school: we had art in the afternoon and we had roast for dinner. Fridays I really didn't like, I was not a lover of fish or of meals without meat. Fish pie, fried fish or cauliflower cheese I could cope with, but cheese flan, oh no!

I have a feeling that this pie is the Marmite of the school pie world. You either loved it or you hated it. I am afraid I fell into the hate camp, but for the sake of authenticity I have recreated it here for the lovers amongst you.

I didn't, however, go hungry on cheese flan days. As the choice on offer was cheese flan or nothing, I took the flan. When no one was looking I'd swap it for a pudding belonging to a cheese-flan lover. So perhaps cheese flan wasn't that bad after all, if it meant double pudding!

Please remember cheese flan must be served with boiled potatoes and tinned tomatoes. Oh, and never, ever, refer to this as a quiche!

✎ Ingredients

150g strong cheddar cheese, grated

1 egg

150 ml milk

Pepper

½ tsp mustard powder

Shortcrust pastry

How to...

1. Preheat the oven to 200°C/Gas 6.
2. Line a small flan ring with pastry and blind bake for 10 minutes. Baking blind means lining the pastry case with baking parchment or grease-proof paper and filling the case with baking beans. Bake, cool slightly and remove the paper and beans.
3. Turn the oven down to 180°C/Gas 4.
4. Mix together the egg, milk, pepper and mustard powder. Stir in the grated cheese. Pour this into the cooled pie case. Make sure the cheese is evenly distributed.
5. Grate a little more cheese over the flan.
6. Bake for 20 minutes until the cheese flan is golden brown on top and has a slight wobble to the filling.
7. Whilst cooking the flan put your new potatoes on to boil and open a tin of tomatoes.

Steak and kidney pudding

Choosing a school coat was fraught with problems. We were told what to wear for school uniform and 'the coat' was our one chance to express our individuality. The problem was we had no desire to be individuals. All of the boys and some of the girls wore parkas; less fortunate individuals had to wear a proper belted macintosh because their mum thought they would last longer. Most feared were the navy quilted anoraks complete with red or blue patterned trim. I would have walked to school coatless in the sleet and snow rather than wear one. Even in the seventies the word 'anorak' was linked to sadness. However hard anyone tried to convince me otherwise, they were never going to be 'in'.

Given the desire of school cooks to fill us so full of stodge we could barely get our parkas done up, it always surprised me that pies only came with tops and never bottoms. In the case of steak and kidney pudding the crust was just like one enormous dumpling – heavenly! This was one of my favourites despite the time it took me to pick out the kidney. I had never liked the texture of kidneys. Eating one reminded me of chewing on the little rubbers at the end of school pencils.

✐ Ingredients

500g stewing steak

125g lamb kidneys

1 onion, finely chopped

Stock

2 tbsp flour

Pepper and salt

Suet pastry

How to...

1. Preheat the oven to 175°C/Gas 4.

2. Cut steak into cubes. Place the flour into a bowl and season well with the salt and pepper. Toss the meat in the flour and coat well. Leave to one side for a few minutes. Trim, core and cube the kidneys.

3. Heat 2 tbsp of oil in a large pan and add the floured beef and the kidneys, then cook until the beef and kidneys are browned. You may need to do this in two batches to prevent the pan from becoming overcrowded. Remove the meats to a large-lidded casserole dish. Add the onion to the frying pan. Continue to cook out until the onion has softened but not taken on any colour.

4. Place the onion into the casserole dish with the steak and kidney. Add the stock to the frying pan and scrape up any sticky bits from the bottom of the pan. Pour the stock from the frying pan into the casserole dish. Put the casserole dish over the heat and bring to simmering point. Reduce the heat right down, cover and leave for half an hour, stirring occasionally.

5. Meanwhile heat the oven to 175°C/Gas 4 and make the suet pastry crust.

6. Remove the casserole from the oven and place the one-piece pie crust on top of the steak and kidney, pressing down to make sure it is in contact with the meat and then replace the casserole lid.

7. Bake for an hour and a half. Do not be tempted to peek or remove the casserole lid as the steam created in the pot will cause the suet crust to rise. If your casserole lid isn't tight fitting seal the edges of the casserole with a flour and water paste.

8. Serve with carrots, peas and thick, thick gravy.

✳ *Variations*

You could make this much more interesting by adding chunks of portobello mushrooms, red wine, stout or even oysters. Try it and see!

Sausage plait

School cooks worked on the principle, 'If it ain't broke don't fix it'. In other words, they fed us meals that were familiar and which they thought were good for us. The lack of choice was not seen as a problem: they were providing a meal and if we didn't eat it we could always become a 'home dinner'. Broccoli, so frequently fed to children now, was nowhere to be seen, sweetcorn came on the cob and beans were runners or baked.

The sausage plait was the first meal to push the boundaries a little. Without question this is simply a sausage roll on steroids. It followed the same basic principle of a pastry case surrounding a sausage interior, but with a few added extras. Including mushrooms was possibly even considered a little racy at the time. Again, sausage plait was always, and inexplicably, served with tinned tomatoes and mash. If the mushrooms were bordering on exotic what they added next was almost unheard of. I am sure this was the first time I ever came across bell peppers or, as our school cook very correctly called them when we pointed and asked 'What's that?', capsicums.

🖉 Ingredients

500g good-quality plain sausages or sausage meat

2 large flat mushrooms, sliced and diced

1 onion, diced

1 egg, beaten

$\frac{1}{2}$ red pepper, finely chopped

Pepper and salt

$\frac{1}{2}$ tsp mustard powder

1 tsp tomato puree

1 tbsp oil

Shortcrust pastry

How to...

1. Preheat the oven to 200°C/Gas 6.
2. In a frying pan heat the oil and add the diced onion. Cook until the onion is softened and has begun to turn golden. Add the mushrooms and cook for a further 5 minutes. Leave to cool for a few moments.
3. Roll out a 25cm by 20cm rectangle of pastry. Put this on to a baking sheet.
4. Place the sausage meat into a large bowl. If you are using sausages split the skins and ease out the sausage meat into a bowl. Season well with salt and pepper; add the mustard powder and tomato puree. Add in the diced red peppers, cooled onion and mushrooms. Using your hands mix together well and place lengthways in the middle of the pastry rectangle.
5. Cut strips 2cm wide in a feather pattern down either side of the pastry. Fold alternating strips across the sausage mixture from top to bottom. Tuck in and tidy the first and last strips, trimming where needed.
6. Brush with the beaten egg and bake for 30 to 35 minutes. If the pastry is browning too quickly, cover with a piece of foil.

✳ Variations

This is lovely eaten cold or at room temperature in the garden on a sunny evening. Please feel free to ignore the previous serving suggestion of tinned toms and mash. I prefer a watercress salad and glass of cold white wine, and so may you!

Pastry would always make an appearance at one course or the other. If it was a tart for pudding then it was not a pie for mains. This didn't mean of course that the meal was any less filling. Casseroles warmed you up, hotpots brought some regionality to the menu and roast dinners were to die for.

Pasta and rice rang the changes on the carbohydrate front, allowing us to feel very cosmopolitan. This exotic move was pushed further with cowboy casserole, spaghetti Bolognaise and chicken curry. Many of the remaining meals were Great British standards like liver and bacon and sausages and mash. Meatballs were sung about, toad in the hole was worried over and spam fritters were raised to iconic status.

Many of these meals relied heavily on tinned tomatoes either as an ingredient or as a garnish, which some people scraped straight into the bin – providing of course they could get under the barbed wire and searchlights that the dinner ladies put up to stop you wasting food. We always suspected they had been trained by foreign governments but no one dared to ask.

* * *

Each recipe makes sufficient for a family of four with some left over for seconds.

Not Pies

Chicken supreme

Cornwall, Dorset, the Norfolk Broads, camping in France or, for the very lucky, a week in Torremolinos. Travelling to these holidays involved long car journeys with the entire contents of your house packed around you, with your grandparents along for good measure. These were the days before the Chelsea tractor, but you would be amazed at how much my parents could shoehorn into a Cortina. Flying to America was out of the question, a complete non-starter, a fact my children find preposterous.

Serving this dish with rice, peas and carrots was the height of cosmopolitan sophistication for our school cook; however, the resulting plate of beige food would probably have sent Jamie Oliver into school-dinner meltdown. We didn't care: chicken supreme was a stirrer's meal. Not because we spent the lunch break whispering behind our hands that Sharon fancied Dave (although we did that too!). Oh no, give us a plate of chicken, rice and vegetables and, providing we didn't get caught, we stirred the whole lot together. Ideally, we would have used just a fork to eat it in the same way as the stars did on American TV programmes such as Little House on the Prairie but we all knew that that was a step too far. Much as we would have liked to see a dinner lady explode it might have delayed our puddings clearing up the resulting mess.

✐ Ingredients

4 chicken breasts or breasts and thighs chunked into cubes

6 medium mushrooms, sliced (use more or less depending on how much you like them)

1 medium onion, finely diced

300ml chicken stock

2 tbsp flour

Salt, pepper, paprika

2 tbsp olive oil

Knob of butter

Lemon

Fresh parsley to serve

How to...

① Heat 1 tbsp of oil and the butter in a pan. Place the flour in a bowl and season well with the salt, pepper and ¼ tsp of paprika. Toss the chicken chunks in the flour, shake off any excess and gently lay in the hot pan. Cook the chicken until golden and crispy on the outside. Do not worry if not completely cooked through yet. Remove to a separate plate and keep warm.

② Add the second tbsp of oil to the pan and tip in the onion. Don't panic if there are still flour bits in the pan, it will help the flavour of the finished dish. Cook the onion until soft and beginning to golden around the edges. Add in the mushrooms and continue cooking until these give out their juices. When this happens add any remaining seasoned flour and cook out for a minute or so, stirring all the time.

③ Pour in the stock and the mixture will thicken slightly. If it thickens too much add a little water or milk at this point.

④ Return the chicken pieces and stir in. Continue cooking for another 5 minutes or until the chicken pieces are cooked through. Taste the sauce and season again. A squeeze of lemon will lift the flavour.

⑤ If beige bothers you please feel free to add baby spinach or peeled and chopped fresh tomatoes at the final moment. Be careful not to cook these to a mush though or the result will be an even nastier colour.

⑥ Serve with rice and vegetables.

⑦ Put on the reruns of *Little House on the Prairie* and eat with just a fork.

Roast dinner

Packed lunches were not an option at my school. You were a school dinner or you were a home dinner. Few and far between, these poor unfortunates (in my nine-year-old opinion) left school when the lunch bell rang and returned for afternoon register. We didn't ask why they went home. I am sure there were valid reasons. Maybe they had medicine to take or perhaps they just preferred their mum's roast potatoes to the ones the school cook made. In my case the opposite was true. My dad made crispy, rough-edged roasties lovingly cooked in beef dripping but I perversely much preferred the drier, soak-up-the-gravy ones we had at school.

Roast dinner was a weekly meal at my school, predictable but oh so comforting. This is not to say that a roast dinner didn't raise our excitement levels. Much discussion was to be had as you neared the tray of meat. Chicken? No, we had that last week. Beef? No, I can't see any Yorkshires. Lamb or pork –must be as I can see a bowl at the end for the sauce. Carrying your plate back to your seat, holding on tight, with your thumb in the gravy, life didn't get much better.

✐ Ingredients

Joint of meat of your choice
Potatoes for roasting, peeled and quartered
Salt and pepper
Vegetable oil, dripping or goose fat
Carrots, peeled and cut into batons or rings
Cabbage, shredded
Gravy
Accompaniments to the meal
(sauces, Yorkshire puddings, etc)

How to...

1. Peel, chop and prepare your vegetables first. Keep them in cold water to prevent discolouration.

2. Put the oven on to heat.

3. Read the label on the joint as almost all supermarkets put oven temperatures and timings on their packaging these days. If you have bought your meat from a butcher ask how long and at what temperature you need to cook your joint. Tell them how you like your meat, still mooing or cremated, and they will give you very good advice.

4. Get a piece of paper if this is your first time cooking a roast and work out your timings. It is not complicated but you must get organised. Write down the cooking time of the meat and add ten minutes' resting time. This is the meat cooking time altogether. Work out when you want to eat and see when the meat must go in to the oven. This is a take-away sum!

5. Potatoes take 50 minutes to 1 hour to roast and need to be par boiled first so will take about 1 hour 20 minutes from preparation to serving. Do another take-away sum now.

6. When ready put the meat in the oven, having seasoned it well with salt and pepper.

7. At the correct time put the potatoes on to boil and also put a large roasting tin containing the fat or oil in the oven. There should be enough fat to cover the bottom of the tin. Once the potatoes come to the boil simmer for 5 minutes and then drain well.

8. Shake the potatoes in the colander – this will get rid of the excess water (water + oil = disaster) and also will roughen the edges to give you crispy spuds. Take the tray from the oven, tip in the potatoes and return to the oven as quickly as possible. You don't want the oil or fat to cool.

9. Open some wine and have a glass – it's going fine so far!

10. The carrots will take 6 or 7 minutes to cook and the cabbage even less.

11. If you want to make your gravy using granules or browning then do – it will give your meal an authentic taste but there is a recipe for proper gravy later in this book.

12. Serve with mint sauce, apple sauce, Yorkshire puddings or mustard as appropriate.

13. Same again next week but using a different joint and what about trying parsnips as well as potatoes?

Toad in the hole

Schools used to be full of animals, of the furry and finned kind you understand. I am not maligning my classmates. The most boring were the fish and the hamsters. Cuddling fish wasn't an option and being nocturnal, hamsters are useless as class pets. Teachers used this nocturnal behaviour to their advantage: we didn't ever see the hamster so when it inevitably popped its clogs a replacement could be bought of any colour or either sex and the class would be none the wiser. Better to have a guinea pig or a rabbit, as they were much more fun.

The annual appearance of frog spawn and tadpoles always meant spring had sprung, quite literally if you left the lid off the tank and the froglets escaped. It did mean you didn't fancy eating one of the best school dinners for a while though.

If this recipe were invented now you would not be allowed to call it toad in the hole. Any school cook would be prosecuted under the Trade Descriptions Act. No toads and no holes, just lots of lovely sausages and crispy batter. This was another meal where lots of swaps went on. You can have my sausage if you give me your batter. Unless of course you were sitting next to me, in which case I tried to persuade you that the sausages really were toads and you refused to eat any of them. Big children can be vile.

🖊 Ingredients

450g good quality chipolata sausages (pack of 12)

1 tbsp oil

125g plain flour

2 eggs

½ pt milk

Salt and pepper

How to...

1. Preheat oven to 240°C/Gas 9. Turn on the grill.
2. Grill the sausages until cooked through.
3. Place a large deep baking tin in the oven with the oil and wait until the pan is smoking hot.
4. Sieve the flour into a large bowl, break in the eggs, add the milk and whisk until combined. Season the batter well.
5. Light a ring on the hob. Take the pan from the oven. Place the pan over the heat and keep hot. Working very quickly, pour the batter into the hot pan and arrange the sausages as evenly as you can.
6. Return the pan to the oven and bake for 20 minutes until risen and golden. Do not peek.
7. Serve with gravy and green beans. You can put these on to boil the day before if you want a retro green bean experience but I suggest a more modern 3 to 5 minutes.

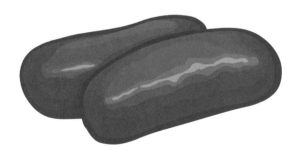

Beef casserole

Seasonality played a part in our school meals. While ice cream and chocolate sauce were served on a hot summer's day, casserole or stew turned up on a cold day, towards the end of a term or half-term when the cook had vegetables to use up. This frugality didn't stop it being delicious. Whilst the basic recipe remained constant, the seasons dictated not only what vegetables went into the dish, but also what accompanied it.

There was almost always cabbage, but still this changed from the crisp and crinkly Savoy via the limp and almost Brussels sprout-flavoured spring greens to the squeaky and very pale hard white cabbage heavily seasoned with white pepper. Not for us deep-frozen broccoli or fine string beans especially flown in from far-away exotic locations. If you couldn't buy it in a sack from the market then we weren't getting it.

Eating beef casserole felt like being hugged from the inside. It was warming and comforting. Easy to eat with mashed potatoes and just now and then, extra gravy. Occasionally if you went up for seconds the hug did tend to squeeze your intestines a little too tightly for the rest of the day. Not that I ever let it put me off my pudding.

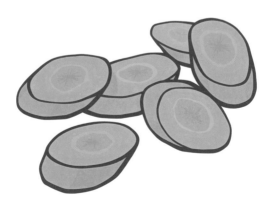

📎 Ingredients

500g stewing steak
1 onion, finely chopped
2 carrots, chopped
Celery, parsnips, swede or whatever is knocking about the
vegetable rack cut to the same size as the carrots
1 tin chopped tomatoes
Water or stock
2 tbsp flour
Pepper and salt
Herbs
Oil
½ tsp sugar

How to...

1. Cut the steak into cubes. Place the flour into a bowl and season well with the salt and pepper. A school cook may have added dried mixed herbs too if she felt she could get away with it. Toss the meat in the flour and coat well. Leave to one side for a few minutes.

2. Heat 2 tbsp of oil in a large pan and add the floured beef, cook until the beef is well browned and then add the onion. Continue to cook out until the onion has softened but not taken on any colour.

3. Add the tin of chopped tomatoes and half a tsp of sugar as this will bring out the tomatoey taste.

4. Add enough stock or water to cover the beef and bring to barely simmering point. Sometimes a squeeze of mustard or a slug of Worcester sauce would make its way in too. Reduce the heat right down, cover and leave for at least 2 hours, stirring occasionally.

5. After 2 hours, check the seasoning and add the carrots and any other vegetables going in. Cover again and leave for a further 30 minutes.

6. Serve from a very large aluminium bowl using a ladle. This always has a scoop of mash and seasonal vegetables to accompany it.

Chicken casserole

Going to school during the fuel crisis of the seventies meant we had to put up with a great deal. But the biggest discomfort for me was when the school canteen was converted from town gas to North Sea gas. Unsurprisingly, this didn't happen in the school holidays but during school term time just to cause maximum disruption. No school dinners for two weeks. We had to take our own lunches. No one had lunch boxes, so we all trooped to and from school clutching our Fine Fare or wavy line plastic bags containing sandwiches wrapped in the waxed bread wrapper, an apple and a slice of cake. After two weeks we were desperate for a hot lunchtime meal and this was what greeted us on that first day back in the canteen.

You knew that it was a special day if this was on the menu. Chicken was a meat saved for occasions: not for us the deep-fried, reconstituted and bright-orange-hued breaded shapes, but real chicken. We knew that because ours came with the skin and bones still attached.

🖉 Ingredients

1 chicken cut into eight portions
(take the skin off if you wish)
1 onion, finely chopped
1 clove garlic
1 carrot, chopped
4 large mushrooms, cut into quarters
4 rashers streaky bacon, chopped
Water or stock
2 tbsp flour
Pepper and salt
Lemon juice
Oil

How to...

① Place flour into a bowl and season well with the salt and pepper. Toss the chicken in the flour and coat well. Leave to one side for a few minutes.

② Heat 2 tbsp of oil in a large pan and add the floured chicken, cook until the chicken pieces have taken on a golden colour. Remove the chicken to a plate and rest. In the chickeny oil cook the bacon until crispy and then add the onion and crushed garlic. Continue to cook until the onion is golden and melting.

③ Add the mushrooms and cook until soft. Tip in any remaining seasoned flour and cook for one minute.

④ Return the chicken to the pan with the bacon, onions and mushrooms.

⑤ Add the stock or water to cover and bring to barely simmering point. Add the carrot. Reduce the heat right down, cover and leave for an hour, stirring occasionally.

⑥ Take a piece of chicken and test that it has cooked through to the bone, check the seasoning. A squeeze of lemon will zing up this dish no end.

⑦ Serve with roast potatoes and bright-green cabbage briefly cooked and still crunchy. Cabbage does not need a fortnight in a nuclear reactor to make it edible. Eat as neatly as you can but suck the bones to get the best bits off if you have to.

Lancashire hotpot

Crusty and brown on the outside and meltingly tender on the inside, Lancashire hotpot was that rare creature: a regional dish on the menu.

Geography at school was spent drawing maps of different places and then spending ages colouring them in. Geography teachers had a real bee in their bonnets about sharp colouring pencils. In a world before photocopiers, laser printers and scanners, our teacher had a huge curved rubber stamp which she rolled over an equally large ink pad. This was placed on to a clean page in your geography book and rolled from top to bottom. Left behind on the page was a faint purple outline of the British Isles. There were similar maps of Europe and The World. Shorelines were shaded in blue colouring pencils and country outlines were shaded according to their sovereignty. Rivers were marked in dark-blue pencil and capitals denoted with a red dot. All this took place without having to engage my brain once.

Consequently I had no idea where Lancashire was but I was eternally grateful to it. Deciding if the potato should be devoured before the meat or after was a dilemma I faced with enthusiasm and a clean plate ready for seconds.

✎ *Ingredients*

750g leg of lamb

2 onions

500 ml water or stock

2 tbsp flour

Pepper and salt

Herbs (thyme if you have it)

Potatoes, thinly sliced (on a mandolin if you are
cavalier about keeping your fingers)

Lidded casserole dish

Oil

Butter

How to...

1. Preheat the oven to 180°C/Gas 4.

2. Cut lamb into cubes. Place the flour into a bowl and season well with the salt and pepper. Toss the meat in the flour and coat well. Leave to one side for a few minutes. The flour is important as it makes your gravy.

3. Slice the onions very finely and mix in with the floured lamb cubes.

4. Place a layer of potato slices in the bottom of your lidded casserole dish or hot pot if you have one. This doesn't have to look beautiful as it is on the bottom!

5. Add in half the lamb and onion mix. Sprinkle in a little thyme at this point. Cover with more potato slices and repeat.

6. When adding the top layer of potato take time to overlap the potato as school cook pride is at stake. Try to make it look reasonably tidy.

7. Add the stock or water until just under the top layer of potatoes. Dot the top with butter or brush the top with a little melted butter. Cover and bake for at least 2 hours.

8. After 2 hours remove the lid and brush or dot again with the butter. Pop under a grill until the top is browned and crispy.

9. Serve from in front of a large map of the UK so everyone knows from whence this wondrous dish originates.

Macaroni cheese

Lunchtime was a dangerous place at school. Twenty-a-side games of football, forty-forty and British bulldog would all carry on at the same time on the same playground, each with their own potential for injury. Small boys in parkas, chosen to play in goal, hurled themselves towards the concrete knowing that the thickness of the parka would save them from broken limbs. The main danger came during sliding tackles as wearing a high proportion of man-made fibres could lead to friction burns or possibly spontaneous combustion.

There was another ball game which involved putting a tennis ball in a stocking, holding on to the open end, leaning against the wall and hitting the ball against the wall as hard as you could. Many a fat lip and bruised cheek resulted from this game and not necessarily your own.

If you had lost teeth, either by natural means or via a rather over-enthusiastic game of British bulldog, macaroni cheese was the meal for you. No chewing at all was required. The slippery cheese sauce and pasta tubes were so soft they could almost be inhaled. To detract from its rather insipid and frankly maggot-like appearance, each portion was adorned with a slice of fresh tomato. However hard you tried to remove the tomato the cheese welded the garnish to the top: a very canny way to get fresh vegetables inside unwilling children!

🖉 Ingredients

125g strong cheddar, grated

25g flour

25g butter

¹/₂ pt milk

375g macaroni

Salt and pepper

Fresh tomato

How to...

1. Preheat the oven to 175°C/Gas 4.
2. Cook the macaroni in salted boiling water until just cooked through. Drain and leave to one side.
3. To make the cheese sauce melt the butter in a large pan, add the flour and cook out for a minute. Add the milk and whisk in to prevent lumps.
4. Cook until the sauce thickens. Once thick, stir in most of the grated cheese. Season to taste.
5. Stir in the macaroni and make sure it is well combined. Tip the mixture into a rectangular baking dish. Scatter over the remaining cheese and garnish each portion with a slice of tomato.
6. Bake in the oven for 20 minutes.
7. Serve with a salad of grated carrot and raisins (I kid you not!).

Cauliflower cheese

School in the seventies had a unique smell for me: a combination of cauliflower, PE kit and tobacco smoke.

Teachers' drawers were always filled with Old Holborn tins, not because they all smoked like chimneys, although given the fug that occasionally leaked out from under the staff-room door many undoubtedly did, but because everyone stored everything in tins. Drawing pins, paperclips and thumbscrews rested safely in the teacher's drawer. Each table had a tin of crayons and we were surprisingly given a tin as soon as we started school containing words we had to learn. Only in the British education system can there be people who, if we ever catch a whiff of roll-up tobacco, instantly think, 'Ah, Janet and John!'

If it was on the menu, you could smell cauliflower cheese as soon as you got to school in the morning. After all, you had to start early to get vegetables that well done. I didn't meet a vegetarian at primary school but if you were then this meal was one of the few choices open to you. The sauce was the best bit and the fact that the cauliflower disintegrated as soon as you put your knife near it only added to the rumour that it was a boiled brain anyway.

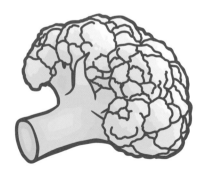

✏ *Ingredients*

125g strong cheddar, grated

25g flour

25g butter

1 tsp dried mustard powder

½ pt milk

1 large cauliflower, cut into florets

4 tbsp fresh breadcrumbs

Salt and pepper

How to...

1. Cook the cauliflower florets in salted boiling water until just cooked. Drain and leave to one side.

2. To make the cheese sauce melt the butter in a large pan, add the flour and mustard powder and cook out for a minute. Add the milk and whisk in to prevent lumps.

3. Cook until the sauce thickens. Once thick, stir in most of the grated cheese. Season to taste.

4. Stir in the cooked cauliflower and make sure it is well combined. Tip the mixture into a rectangular baking dish. Scatter over the remaining cheese and breadcrumbs.

5. Flash under the grill until the cheese bubbles and the breadcrumbs are toasted.

6. Serve as a side dish with pork chops or eat as a main meal with a big green salad.

Baked fish and parsley sauce

Having visitors at school always led to a certain amount of dashing about and excitement. It led to confusion too as the word 'visitors' was often used as a euphemism for head lice.

Sometimes the visitor was the school nurse giving the 'growing up' talk. Occasionally it was a school inspector who was shown around a suddenly very tidy and well-behaved school by the head teacher. Perhaps the local policeman had come in to remind us to join the Tufty club and cross roads safely. Best of all was the visitor to assembly. Many churches sent youth workers into school to share the good news with the great unwashed. The message completely passed us by on most occasions but the joy of singing a hymn to the tune of Match of the Day made our assembly. The guitar-playing young man went away happy to have touched our lives and we were just pleased not to have to sing 'All things bright and beautiful' for the third time that week.

If it's Friday it must be fish. All schools, religious or not, kept this tradition going. It looked very anaemic and quite frankly boring, but do not be deceived. Fish also meant peas and potatoes in some form or other. These came mashed, chipped, mushy or boiled and were only there to soak up the best bit – the parsley sauce. Cod, or more often coley or whiting – it didn't matter; just take care not to swallow any bones.

✐ Ingredients

Fish	Sauce
600–800g firm white fish fillets	300 ml milk
Butter	Fish cooking juices
Lemon juice	40g butter
300ml milk	40g flour
Salt and pepper	Fresh parsley, chopped

How to...

1. Preheat oven to 200°C/Gas 6.
2. Butter an oven-proof dish and lay the fish fillets in the dish. Squeeze a little lemon over the fish and season well with salt and pepper.
3. Pour the milk into the dish to surround the fish. Take a sheet of greaseproof paper and cover the fish and milk.
4. Bake in the oven for 20 minutes or until the fish is just cooked. Carefully remove the fish to a warmed plate and strain the cooking liquid into a jug.
5. Make the sauce by melting the butter in a pan. Stir in the flour and cook out for a minute but do not brown. Add the cooking liquid a little at a time until the sauce is the consistency of double cream. You may need to use some of the extra milk at this point.
6. Stir in the chopped parsley.
7. Place a fish fillet on a plate and pour over the parsley sauce. Serve with mash and peas. A wedge of lemon would be nice too. Oh, and a green salad and a glass of cold Pinot Grigio. See, fish doesn't have to be boring at all!

Spam fritters

Surely this has to be the guiltiest pleasure of them all. To be perfectly honest it was the batter that did it for me. Just writing this recipe I can feel my arteries furring up and my cholesterol level moving skywards.

Not that we had fried food very often, there seems to be a myth that has grown up suggesting we ate chips all the time but from the other recipes in this book you can see this is plainly not true. They were probably as rare for us as they are for present-day consumers of school dinners. Mind you, we did have fried fish and doughnuts too, but again these were an occasional treat.

This is one of those things that people profess not to like but secretly enjoy. A bit like putting a CD of eighties power ballads on in the car and then claiming they belong to your partner.

Whilst not confessing to a love of Bonnie Tyler, I would gladly shout from the rooftops that I love spam fritters. Strangely, plain cold and straight from the tin spam doesn't do it for me; it has to have a crispy coat and be blisteringly hot before I entertain eating it.

Everything in moderation is fine, so enjoy this culinary treat, just not too often!

✐ *Ingredients*

1 can of spam
100g plain flour
Pinch of salt
Ice cold sparkling mineral water
Flour for dusting
Oil for frying

How to...

1. Place the spam tin into the refrigerator to chill for several hours before starting this recipe.

2. Remove the spam from the tin and slice into 1cm thick portions. Place back into the fridge until needed.

3. Mix together the flour and sparkling mineral water until the batter is the thickness of double cream. If you don't have sparkling mineral water add 1 tsp of bicarbonate of soda to the flour instead. The secret to this batter is to use ice-cold water. Add a pinch of salt.

4. Put the oil on to heat. You can shallow or deep fry depending on your bravery or your equipment.

5. Take the spam out of the fridge and coat very lightly in flour. Remove any excess by patting the spam gently. The flour will help the batter to stick. Dip the spam into the batter and lay gently into the oil. The oil needs to be fairly hot or your batter will become soggy.

6. The fritters will take about 2 minutes on each side and about 3 or 4 minutes if you are deep frying. Remove from the oil when golden brown. Drain well.

7. Serve with mash and beans or peas. Ketchup is an optional accompaniment.

Spaghetti Bolognaise

The seventies are sometimes accused of being the decade that fashion forgot. I'd dispute that, I think it is the decade we all wish fashion had forgotten. We embraced every bizarre clothing style that the seventies had to offer, had our photographs taken and have been trying to destroy the evidence ever since.

If you know anyone who married during this time I bet they don't have a single wedding photo on public display. Looking at these images has given my children hours of fun and not inconsiderable pain from laughing so much. Why is the sight of your mum, aged 11, wearing a wide-brimmed floppy hat, long dress and carrying a crochet shoulder bag so hilarious? Thank goodness they haven't seen the catsuit photo.

It has to be remembered that when we had spag bol at school it was the most sophisticated dish on the planet even if we said it did look like dirt and worms. Imagine sushi being served in state primary schools today and you get the gist of the cutting edge we were at. The only details missing were the checked tablecloths and the Chianti bottle with a candle in it. For some peculiar reason the pasta was chopped up into 4 inch lengths and stirred into the sauce before serving. Despite being that quintessential Italian dish, ours was always served with carrots and peas.

🖉 Ingredients

1 onion, chopped

500g lean mince (lamb or beef)

Chopped tomatoes (always tinned in a school meal!)

Several diced carrots – don't ask me why
but they were ever present

A few dried mixed herbs

Slug of Worcester sauce

Salt and pepper

Stock

Dried spaghetti – for true authenticity
use the long pasta in the blue paper packet,
as it was the only one in the sixties and seventies

How to...

1. Brown the onion in a saucepan and then add the carrots.
2. Tip in the minced beef or lamb and cook until mince is no longer in lumps.
3. Stir in the tinned tomatoes, herbs, Worcester sauce and seasoning.
4. Cover with stock (school cooks may just have used water or cabbage water!). Bring to the simmer and reduce the heat until the surface of the mince mixture just quivers.
5. Leave to cook for at least 2 hours, stirring occasionally. Add more water only if needed. I think the key to this mince recipe was long slow cooking! I know we have all heard the jokes about the food in school kitchens being put on a low gas at 9am to serve at 12.30 but in this case it would have made the difference. It is the way the Italians have been making good ragu for years.

❋ Variations

Occasionally if the pasta was too exhausting there was a British version of this dish.

1. *Cut the crust off a slice of bread and cut into four triangles. Heat lard or bacon fat in a pan until very hot and then fry the bread. Hot fat will soak in less than cool fat.*
2. *Place the mince in an oblong metal tray. Place the fried bread attractively over the mince (one per portion). Ring the bell and off you go.*

Meatballs

A meal so revered they wrote a song about it: 'On top of spaghetti, all covered in cheese, I once lost my meatball when somebody sneezed.'

Meatballs were one of the few main elements of a meal to come out of a tin. Usually they had a tomato sauce but occasionally they arrived in gloopy gravy. Very, very rarely – I suspect if there were not enough tins of either one or the other type of meatball – you ended up with a combination of the two: a sort of meaty tomatoey jollop. Surprisingly, this wasn't as nasty as it could have been.

Portion control for meatballs involved counting them on to the plate. Engaging the dinner lady in conversation could, if you were lucky, result in a miscount and an extra meatball on your plate. Infants got fewer than juniors too. Parmesan wasn't available for sprinkling, though you might get grated cheddar if you were lucky.

The spaghetti could be a problem. It sometimes stuck together in clumps and had to be cut into wedges for serving. We didn't really mind: presentation was not a huge issue for us. Taste and quantity were far more important.

A meatball was small enough to eat whole but too big to allow a conversation to continue without pebble dashing your friend with tomato sauce. If anyone told a joke then the entire table resembled a massacre. Just brilliant.

✏️ Ingredients

Meatballs

500g lean mince (lamb or beef)
100g fresh breadcrumbs
100g finely grated cheddar cheese
A few dried mixed herbs
1 egg, beaten
Salt and pepper
Oil for frying

Sauce

Stock
400g sieved tomatoes (passata)

How to...

1. In a large bowl combine all the meatball ingredients together until well mixed.
2. Using damp hands pinch off walnut-sized pieces of mixture and roll to create ball shapes. Place to one side until all the meatballs are made.
3. Heat a tablespoon of oil in a large frying pan and add the meatballs to the pan. Do not move in the pan for five minutes otherwise your meatballs will disintegrate. Turn gently every few minutes until all the sides are browned.
4. Once the meatballs are browned add 300ml of passata (you can push a can of tomatoes through a sieve if you are feeling either butch or masochistic but I wouldn't bother) and enough stock to just come half way up your balls.
5. Simmer gently for 20 minutes until the meatballs are cooked through.
6. Serve with spaghetti and grated cheese so you can sing the song or boiled potatoes and greens if you don't want the musical accompaniment.

Liver and bacon

Technically this dish is not liver and bacon but liver with bacon. Seeing rolls of crispy bacon lined up on the silver tray made my heart leap knowing that liver was on the menu. Others in school were less enthusiastic. Their revulsion usually began after thinking too hard about the ingredients involved in this meal. Personally I didn't let this bother me.

The thick tasty gravy coating the ever present mash had a depth of flavour unparalleled in other school meals. The glutton in me also knew that seconds of the liver were always going to be forthcoming and if I was lucky the bacon too.

Handled badly liver could very quickly resemble shoe leather both in texture and shape. We were very fortunate to have a cook who knew that care had to be taken. She wanted us to eat the food she prepared and made a huge effort to make liver and bacon a meal that was tolerated at worst and positively loved at best. School cooks didn't have time to lovingly sauté the liver briefly as is so popular today. They resorted to the long slow cook of the casserole and very effective it was too.

Ingredients

500g lambs' or calves' liver, sliced thinly

1 onion, finely chopped

350ml vegetable or chicken stock

2 tbsp flour

250g streaky bacon

Pepper and salt

Herbs, dried mixed (very seventies!) or fresh

Oil

Knob of butter

How to...

1. Preheat the oven to 150°C/Gas 2.

2. In the past liver was soaked in milk to temper the stronger flavours, especially from pigs' or ox liver. If you want to do this that is fine, especially if cooking for liver virgins, but it shouldn't be necessary for school-dinner veterans.

3. Trim the liver, removing any tubes or membrane. I don't want to put you off but they can be very chewy. Slice into thin escalopes if you want this school-cook style or just cut into 1cm thick slices.

4. Place the flour, salt, pepper and herbs on to a plate. Coat the liver slices in the flour, patting off the excess. Heat the knob of butter and 1 tbsp of oil in a pan. Fry the liver briefly to give the liver a golden crust. Place the liver in a casserole dish.

5. Fry the onion in the same pan, adding a little more oil if you need to. Once the onion has softened and browned add in any remaining flour and cook for a further minute. Pour in the stock and stir until this mixture thickens slightly.

6. Pour the thickened stock over the liver in the casserole dish and top up with a little more stock to barely cover if needed.

7. Place the lid on and cook for an hour and a half.

8. Whilst the casserole is cooking make the streaky bacon rolls. Using the back of a knife stretch the rashers until twice their original length. Cut each rasher in half and roll up into a cylinder.

9. Place on a baking tray. With half an hour to go place these rolls in the oven to bake alongside the liver and onions.

10. Serve the liver slices with a big scoop or two of creamy mash smothered with thick tasty gravy and a streaky bacon roll on the side. Seconds anyone?

Chicken curry

Eating out for my family was a very special treat. It usually consisted of a meal of steak, chips and peas at the local Berni Inn. The highlight of this meal was a heart-shaped raspberry-ripple choc ice for pudding. Fish and chips came from the take away and very occasionally you might have a Chinese meal. My parents went out to an Italian trattoria or French bistro with friends for celebration meals.

We didn't do spicy food. Worcester sauce and English mustard were the hottest tastes we would contemplate. Slowly, though, we began to have our taste buds tickled by new flavours and experiences and surprisingly the school cook played her part. Until boil in the bag Vesta curry was invented, school chicken curry was as close as it got. There is nothing remotely authentic about this dish at all but it still tasted wonderful. It was looked forward to if only for the rice which gave us a sticky change from potatoes. The rice was served into the middle of the plate and the back of a large aluminium ladle was applied to the centre of the rice to form a well. Using the same ladle the curry was deposited into this well with the minimum of ceremony and often from a great height.

✎ Ingredients

4 chicken breasts cut into cubes

1 onion, finely chopped

1 clove garlic

1 apple, peeled and chopped

1 handful of raisins

1 to 1½ tbsp curry powder (your choice of strength)

Water or stock

2 tbsp flour

Pepper and salt

Lemon juice

Oil

How to...

1. Place flour into a bowl and season well with the salt and pepper. Toss the chicken in the flour and coat well. Leave to one side for a few minutes.

2. Heat 2 tbsp of oil in a large pan and add the floured chicken, cook until the chicken pieces have taken on a golden colour. Remove the chicken to a plate and rest. Add the onion and crushed garlic to the chickeny oil. Continue to cook until the onions are golden and melting.

3. Add in the curry powder and cook out until the spices are no longer raw. Return the chicken to the pan with the apple and the raisins.

4. Add enough stock or water to cover the meat and bring to barely simmering point. Reduce the heat right down, cover and leave for half an hour stirring occasionally.

5. Take a piece of chicken and test that it has cooked through and check the seasoning. A quick squeeze of lemon isn't authentic but may help cut the sweetness a little.

6. Serve with rice and ladle the curry into the middle from enough height that you might get froth on it.

Cowboy casserole

Not made with cowboys, although I did go through a rather traumatic period when I though shepherd's pie was made with shepherds!

Cowboy casserole is one of those meals designed to fill you up and keep you going. It was also one of those few school meals that were given a slightly fanciful name. School cooks and dinner ladies didn't have time to chat. Call a meal beef casserole and you know what you are getting. Calling it something obtuse means you have to keep answering the 'What's in it?' question.

Cowboy casserole was a dish that gave us aspirations. Eat this and you too could ride across the plains rounding up cattle and fending off attacks from bows and arrows. I wasn't that interested in any cowboys packing six shooters. The cowboy of my dreams rode into our lives during the Magpie advert breaks.

I lived in hope that one day the Milky Bar Kid would wander in and serve this to us. Why on earth I imagined he would do that in a South London primary school eludes me now but I suspect it may have been my hormones talking. For many of us he was a first crush, In fact, even now, there are fewer things more alluring than a man with an endless supply of chocolate.

✐ Ingredients

450g good quality chipolata sausages
1 large onion, finely chopped,
1 tin baked beans
1 tin chopped tomatoes
3 tbsp oil
Flour
Salt and pepper
Worcester sauce
300 ml stock or water
2 large baking potatoes

How to...

1. Preheat oven to 200°C/Gas 6.
2. Grill the sausages until cooked through. Cut each sausage into three or four pieces and place in the casserole dish.
3. Peel and chop the potatoes into crouton-sized cubes. Toss in 1 tbsp of the oil and season well. Set aside.
4. Finely slice the onion and fry gently in the remaining oil until softened. Add flour a tablespoon at a time and mix in until all the oil is absorbed. Allow this mixture to cook out for at least 1 minute. Add the stock and cook out again until the mixture thickens.
5. Pour the onion sauce over the sausages and add the tomatoes and beans. Season with salt, pepper and Worcester sauce to taste.
6. Scatter the surface of the casserole with the potato chunks and bake in the oven for 30 to 40 minutes, or until the potatoes are cooked through.
7. Best eaten with a hat on the side of your head whilst dreaming of wide open spaces and white chocolate!

Sausages and mash

Hardly a recipe really, this was the closest that school cooks came to a ready meal. The sausages just needed frying or, in most cases, baking in the oven, the potatoes were peeled and mashed and the tins of beans were opened using the largest tin openers I have ever seen in my entire life. They were attached to the wall and had what looked like a lethal prong on them that was used to impale and open the industrial quantities of beans needed to keep us all full.

No one needed to encourage us to eat bangers, beans and mash by forming mountains with the mash and using the beans to create lava flows. Pleasure came in the form of the school sausages that had a seriously crispy outside with a soft pink interior. Add to these two scoops of mash, if you were polite to the dinner lady, and a ladleful of beans: bliss!

Happiness didn't always come from the meal alone. Of course bangers, beans and mash led to the singing of the now legendary, 'Beans, beans, good for your heart' song in the queue. I know of no one who got to the 'f' word without being led firmly to the back of the line. The no singing at the table rule must have been invented for bangers, beans and mash.

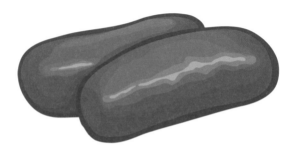

✏ Ingredients

Sausages

Beans

4 to 6 large floury potatoes

Knob of butter

Milk 3 to 4 tablespoons

Salt and pepper

How to...

1. Preheat the oven to 200°C/Gas 6.
2. Peel and chop the potatoes into cubes and place into a pan of cold salted water. Bring the water to the boil and simmer until the potatoes are soft.
3. Put the sausages into a large baking dish and bake for 20 minutes for chipolatas and 30 minutes for thicker sausages.
4. In a small pan warm the milk but don't boil it and then remove from the heat.
5. Drain the potatoes and leave to steam for a minute or so otherwise the mash will be very soggy. Using a potato masher or ricer, mash the spuds well ensuring there are no lumps.
6. Stir in the warmed milk until you have the consistency of mash you like. Add a knob of butter and season to taste.
7. If you like beans, open a can, heat and serve with the sausages and mash. Gravy is an alternative accompaniment.

Fried fish and chips

Comics were the reading material of choice for many of us. Beano, Dandy, Twinkle and Bunty relieved us of our pocket money on a regular basis. Twinkle and Bunty were a little sedate for my liking although I quite enjoyed the paper doll on the back page which I would cut out weekly and customise with my 60 pack of Woolworths felt pens.

Beano and Dandy were much more fun, full of practical jokes, inspiring us to get up to no good. We loved playing tricks on each other. Surprisingly, fish and chips allowed us to indulge in this practical joking even further.

This was the Friday fish dish we looked forward to the most. The batter was always crispy but the chips were often soggy due to the quantities they were cooked in and the time they spent crowded together for warmth in those large-lidded aluminium trays.

Never mind, this was the day we got salt and vinegar on the tables and tomato sauce too! Leaving the lids unscrewed for the next unsuspecting victim to cover themselves in condiments was a joy in itself.

Ingredients

Fish

4 firm white fish fillets

200g plain flour

250ml ice-cold water

Seasoned flour for dusting

Oil for frying (groundnut or beef dripping
if being very authentic)

Chips

4 to 6 large floury potatoes

How to...

1. Heat the oil in a deep saucepan until very hot.
2. Slice the potatoes into your favoured chip size.
3. Mix together the flour and iced water using a whisk. Use elbow grease to knock out any lumps. Turn the fish fillets in the seasoned flour and pat off any excess.
4. Before the oil reaches its maximum heat cook the chips until soft but not coloured at all. Drain and cool on kitchen paper.
5. Once the oil is very hot dip the fish fillet into the batter and lay in the oil without causing any splashes. Cook for 4 to 5 minutes, until the batter is cooked. The fish will have steamed inside the batter in this time. Drain and keep warm.
6. Return the partly cooked chips to the very hot oil for another few minutes until crispy and golden brown.
7. Drench with salt and vinegar whilst still hot and add a dollop of ketchup if you like.

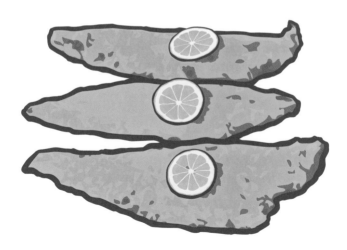

School puddings are the stuff of legends. Gather together enough people who remember space hoppers the first time round, open a bottle of wine and they will gladly tell you about their favourite school puddings.

For many people the main reason for having school dinners was the puddings. From Great British standards such as Jam roly-poly and apple pie to unique school puddings like butterscotch tart and cornflake cake, school cooks the nation over added to the excitement in the dinner hall daily. Custards of various colours and flavours flowed freely. Seasonal fruits added to the variety of foods on offer and dried fruits maintained a regularity that was essential to all. Puddings were sung about and remembered in poems, so vital were they to our lives.

Try these recipes to tempt the taste buds of your nearest and dearest. Don't forget the custard, and can I have the skin please?

* * *

Each of these recipes makes enough for a family of four with plenty left over for seconds.

Puddings

Manchester tart

Hot days at school seemed to last for ever. They weren't helped by the way the buildings were built with large almost floor-to-ceiling windows. Somehow the school's orientation meant that the sun shone constantly on the school windows and these windows focused all the light and heat on to the classroom inhabitants.

Only the upper window panes could be tilted open at a minuscule angle. A faint waft of air might reach you eventually but to call it a breeze would lead to action under the Trade Descriptions Act. Asking to get a drink of water was frowned upon. Had we asked for Cresta perhaps we would have had more chance of slaking our thirsts. So we sat and poached slowly in our own rapidly reducing liquid, dreaming of the day when all school children would have water bottles on their tables.

Naming this 'Manchester tart' defies logic. Even with the scares recently over climate change I have never heard of the coconut being native to Manchester. This is a fantastic way to use up leftover pastry, jam and custard. Actually, what I have written there is tantamount to heresy. Fancy suggesting there could be such a thing as leftover custard.

I am sure that just reading the name on the menu gave adolescents up and down the country the opportunity to laugh at the double entendre.

✏️ Ingredients

Pastry
250g plain flour
125g butter or margarine
Cold water

Filling
Jam (red!)
Custard powder
1 pint milk
Desiccated coconut
Sugar

How to...

1. Preheat oven to 200°C/Gas 6.
2. Follow the instructions for pastry given in the cornflake tart recipe.
3. Roll out the pastry; line a tin 14 inches by 8 inches. Prick with a fork, fill with baking beans and bake blind for 15 minutes. Remove the baking beans and bake for a further 5 minutes. Allow to cool.
4. Turn the oven down to 170°C/Gas 4.
5. Once cool spread the pastry case with the jam of your choice. For both looks and ease of eating I suggest something red and seedless, but the choice is yours.
6. Make up custard according to makers instructions and allow to cool slightly. Pour the custard over the jammy base and sprinkle with the coconut. This will prevent a skin forming on the custard as well as giving a lovely taste.
7. Cool completely and serve with cream or more custard if you can stomach it.

Banana flan

School-dinner ladies had endless variations on the tart. This is not meant as a sleight on their good character. Dinner ladies were nothing if not the most upstanding members of the school community. Often they were relatives of your friends, so to call their morality into question could often lead to a Chinese burn or worse.

Dinner-lady uniform also made the most voluptuous of women look like Russian shot-putters at the Munich Olympics. The hairnet with its white brim pushed the brow down and gave all dinner ladies that thoroughly fed-up expression; at least I think it was the hairnet that did it. Over this went what my nan would call a pinny, but was more properly called a tabard. The school cook got to wear a button-up white coat and, if they so chose, a white acrylic trilby. They looked efficient but scary. Thinking about it, putting that quantity of nylon into a kitchen nowadays would cause a health and safety implosion; I am just surprised there were not more school cooks catching fire.

Whatever they wore, the proof of the pudding, as they say, is in the eating. This banana flan is a good way to use up the slightly overripe bananas that lurk in the bottom of the fruit bowl. I am sure this was an economically driven pudding using up excess pastry, jam tarts or bananas. Banana flan tastes great with butterscotch sauce too.

✏ *Ingredients*

Pastry	Filling
250g plain flour	Jam (red!)
125g butter or margarine	Custard powder
Cold water	1 pint milk
	Sugar
Or use a ready-made	Bananas
sponge-flan case	Desiccated coconut

How to...

1. Preheat oven to 200°C/Gas 6.
2. If you have had enough of pastry please use a sponge-flan case for this recipe.
3. Follow the instructions for pastry given in the cornflake tart recipe.
4. Roll out the pastry; line a tin 14 inches by 8 inches. Prick with a fork, fill with baking beans and bake blind for 15 minutes. Remove the baking beans and bake for a further 5 minutes. Allow to cool.
5. Once cool, spread the pastry case with the jam of your choice.
6. Slice the bananas and place over the jam. Be as generous as you like with the bananas.
7. Make up custard according to maker's instructions and allow to cool slightly. Pour the custard over the bananas. Sprinkle with sugar and desiccated coconut. This will prevent a skin forming on the custard as well as giving a lovely taste.
8. Cool completely and serve with cream.

❊ *Variations*

You can substitute the custard in this recipe for the butterscotch mixture from the butterscotch tart recipe. This makes a fantastic banoffee pudding. Serve with cream or hot custard.

Jam tart
(and traffic-light tart)

Wearing school uniform seemed to be an optional extra at my primary school. We had school colours and so long as your jumper, cardigan or summer dress fitted vaguely in with these then that would be fine. Not that there was much choice in style or design. Pinafores had box pleats, shirts had cuffs and buttons and all shoes had a t-bar and buckles.

Secondary school was a little stricter, with jumpers in one colour, skirts and shirts from a particular shop and shoes with a low heel. We all looked as if we belonged, but we were not clones. Schools expected the rules to be kept but didn't stipulate the vast number of logo-bearing items that exist on uniform lists today. Quite how the behaviour policy of a school will implode because your child doesn't have a pair of PE shorts bearing the school Latin motto is beyond me. Keeping it plain and simple always works for me.

In the recipe below the school cooks followed this rule, classic and very simple, but that didn't detract from my love of the jam tart. I always wanted a piece from the middle (more jam and less pastry!).

I was less fond of traffic-light tart, a kaleidoscope of red, orange and green blobs, which I now see was just an excuse to use up the scrapings from the bottom of half-used pots of jam. The game was to get a piece with all three colours on, but I was never very successful.

Serve with custard and, yes, I do want the skin please!

🔖 *Ingredients*

Pastry
250g plain flour
125g butter or margarine
Cold water

Filling
Jam (red and seedless)
(For traffic lights you need red,
orange and green jam or marmalade)

How to...

1. Preheat oven to 200°C/Gas 6.
2. Follow the instructions for pastry given in the cornflake tart recipe.
3. Roll out the pastry; line a tin 14 inches by 8 inches. Prick with a fork, fill with baking beans and bake blind for 15 minutes. Remove the baking beans and bake for a further 5 minutes. Allow to cool.
4. Turn the oven down to 170°C/Gas 4.
5. Once cool, spread the pastry case with the jam of your choice. For both looks and ease of eating I suggest something red and seedless but if you want to make traffic-light tart use a red, orange and green filling: the choice is yours.

Cornflake tart

School cooking lessons in primary school seemed to lead to one of three outcomes: fairy cakes, gingerbread men or chocolate Easter nests. The first came with icing, the second with currants and a thin slither of glacé cherry and the third and final came with one foil-wrapped chocolate egg. All very predictable, as was the fact that if you caught the bus home any cakes you had left in your tin would be devoured by the bus bully.

At secondary school cooking was eclectic to say the least; we made rock buns one week and a Swiss roll the next, neither of which I have had much call to bake since. The one real skill I was left with was learning how to make Tupperware 'burp' to prevent spillage from the container on the way home.

I wish to goodness that I had learned to cook cornflake tart at school. Since creating this recipe I have had requests to make it often. Golden and sparkly, this pudding was the jewel in the crown, the treasure at the end of the rainbow, or at the very least the reward for eating up all your liver and onions. Cornflake tart is a true gangster's moll of tarts, a deep crusty initially unyielding exterior with a surprisingly sweet layer inside.

✐ Ingredients

Pastry

250g plain flour
125g butter or margarine
Cold water

Filling

Jam (red!)

Cornflake topping

125g caster sugar
125g butter
220g cornflakes
125g golden syrup

How to...

1. Preheat oven to 200°C/Gas 6.

2. Place flour and fat into a large bowl and rub in the fat until the mixture resembles breadcrumbs. Using a round-bladed knife stir in the cold water a little at a time until the mixture begins to come together. Use your hands to form a ball of pastry. Wrap the pastry in cling film and rest for half an hour or so in the fridge. (If this is too much trouble then buy the pastry – no one will ever know!)

3. Roll out the pastry; line a tin 14 inches by 8 inches. Prick with a fork, fill with baking beans and bake blind for 15 minutes. Allow to cool.

4. Turn the oven down to 170°C/Gas 4.

5. Once cool, spread the pastry case with the jam of your choice. For both looks and ease of eating I suggest something red and seedless but the choice is yours.

6. Place the sugar, syrup and butter in a large pan and heat gently until the butter has melted. Give the mixture a good stir and add in the cornflakes a few handfuls at a time until either the cornflakes are all added or the toffee mixture is all used up. Mix well to make sure each cornflake is sticky. I generally test this by having a quick spoonful but be careful as hot sugar burns!

7. Place the cornflake mix into the jammy tart case and press down well with the back of a spoon to compress and smooth the surface. Bake in the oven for 10 minutes. Take out and cool. When absolutely cold use a serrated knife to cut into squares. The size of each square depends upon whether you are cutting a piece for yourself or someone else, I usually find.

8. For a full school-dinner effect serve with pink custard.

Jam roly-poly

It is a little-known fact that small children believe they are made from rubber. This has led to children in playgrounds up and down the land contorting their bodies in an unimaginable number of ways.

This party trick would be shared first with friends and, if good enough, audiences would be gathered to 'ooh', 'aah' and generally be revolted. Anyone who was 'double-jointed' would point fingers in strange directions and make their thumbs touch their forearms with ease. Some children could skip using their arms instead of ropes. As we moved closer to Halloween older boys would turn their eyelids inside out to scare the younger children. Rarely, these party pieces would result in an accident and true to gruesome form we would all have a good look at the injury before summoning help.

Jam roly-poly always looked like one of these playground accidents but it didn't bother us much. In fact, it was often given a blood-curdling nickname to match. What a pudding jam roly-poly was: it was as capable of keeping you warm as a balaclava helmet and mittens on strings. Volcanically hot jam tempered by the soft suet crust and the ever-present custard. Occasionally the syrup sponge roll would make an appearance just in case we began to feel our sugar levels drop.

✏ Ingredients

75g suet

150g flour

1tsp baking powder

Cold water

4 tbsp seedless jam (raspberry or strawberry)

How to...

1. Preheat the oven to 200°C/Gas 6.
2. Using a round-bladed knife mix together the dry ingredients. Adding a little water at a time bring together the mixture to form a soft dough. Use your hands to lift the mixture from the bowl and shape gently into a ball.
3. Roll or pat out the dough until it is a rectangle about 8 inches by 12 inches or 20 by 30cm.
4. Spread the dough with the jam. Dampen the edges with water or milk. Roll the dough into a log shape and place in a lightly buttered baking tin.
5. Bake for 30 to 40 minutes until risen and golden.
6. Serve with lashings of custard and extra warmed jam if so desired.

✳ Variations

For a steamed or baked syrup sponge roll substitute the jam for the same quantity of golden syrup. Into the golden syrup add a couple of tablespoons of fresh white breadcrumbs. This helps the syrup to stay put in the roll and not escape all over the baking tray when heated.

Arctic roll

Each season, and there were four proper ones in the sixties and seventies, was very different. The weather and consequently your clothing changed; the vegetables we ate in the dinner hall varied; even the contents of pockets had seasonality. Spring brought eggshells in pastel colours collected from the pavement or possibly out of nests. Summer meant bugs and creepy crawlies imprisoned in a Swan Vesta box with a leaf for company. Autumn's collection consisted of conkers, acorns and sycamore keys, ready to be fought with or spun down to earth in timed competitions. Winter's contributions were twigs and stones, elastic bands dropped by the postman and endless pieces of string.

I know that you can buy a perfectly good Arctic roll but I thought I'd quite like to make one from scratch. Not that any self-respecting dinner lady would have done this, but if you want to impress your guests here goes...

Ingredients

100g caster sugar (but don't put it away
you will need to sprinkle some later)
100g self-raising flour
4 large eggs
1 tub vanilla ice cream (not soft scoop)
Raspberry jam

How to...

1. Preheat your oven to 220°C/Gas 7.

2. Line a Swiss roll tin with baking parchment.

3. Lay out a sheet of baking parchment the length of your Swiss roll tin. Take scoops of the vanilla ice cream and lay them down the length of this paper. You should now have a log of vanilla ice cream. Roll up the paper tightly to give you a vanilla ice cream sausage. This will become the centre of your Arctic roll. Place in the freezer until really solid.

4. Now to make the sponge. Place the eggs and sugar into a bowl and whisk together so that they become light in colour and very foamy. If you lift the whisk you should see a trail left behind.

5. Sift in the flour and using a metal spoon and a cutting action mix in carefully.

6. Pour the sponge mix into your tin and gently tip it to move the mix into every corner of the tin.

7. Bake for 10 to 12 minutes or until golden brown.

8. Take another, yes another, piece of baking parchment just longer than your Swiss roll tin (you may not be that accurate in your cake tipping!). If you don't have enough paper you can use a clean tea towel for this too. Sprinkle your parchment or tea towel with a generous amount of caster sugar. Turn your sponge out onto the caster sugary surface. Allow to cool slightly.

9. Spread generously with jam. Remove your vanilla ice cream sausage from the freezer.

10. Unwrap and place along one long side of the sponge. Roll the sponge around the ice cream, using the paper or towel to help. Once rolled, wrap in cling film and replace in the freezer. Remove 20 minutes before serving and place in the fridge to soften slightly.

11. Seemingly always served with tinned mandarins, but you choose. Fresh soft fruit might complement all your hard work a little more elegantly.

Spotted dick

Everyone had a nickname whether they knew it or not. The majority of these nicknames were derived from surnames or, occasionally physical attributes, 'Chalky White' and 'Lanky' being amongst the most obvious, although to this day I am not sure why anyone called Clarke gets landed with the epithet 'Nobby'. Children, sometimes having a cruel sense of humour, would also use the exact opposites for nicknames; as a consequence, there would be a look of surprise on people's faces when introduced to 'Shorty' or 'Slim'!

Teachers were far from immune. Almost all teachers and dinner ladies had a nickname. These names were never ever used to address them in person unless you had a sudden rush of blood to the head and totally forgot yourself. Teacher and dinner-lady nicknames usually picked up on a physical quirk or a character trait and targeted those.

Apparently 'spotted dick' now goes by the name of 'spotted dog'. Really, do we need to be that PC about things; life is full of jokes and double entendres, not always in good taste. This taught us that if you laughed too loudly you may have to explain to everyone in the queue exactly what you found so funny. Giggle inwardly and get over it.

✏️ *Ingredients*

75g flour
80g suet
1 tsp baking powder
100g fresh breadcrumbs
60g soft brown sugar
150g currants or raisins (soaked in cold tea or water); if
you like more spots then do add more soaked fruit
60 ml milk (depending on the flour and breadcrumbs
you may need a little more)

How to...

1. Using a round-bladed knife mix together the dry ingredients. Stir in the soaked currants. Adding a little milk at a time, bring together the mixture to form a soft dough. Use your hands to lift the mixture from the bowl and gently shape into a log.

2. Lay out a sheet of greaseproof paper long enough to go around the pudding at least twice. Pleat the paper several times to allow for the pudding to expand.

3. Wrap up the pudding and repeat using foil, pleating again to prevent explosions.

4. Seal well and lower into simmering water. Simmer for 90 minutes. Remove carefully and drain. Open carefully as steam burns. Slice and serve with custard, cream or ice cream.

Butterscotch tart

Life as a teacher's pet was something of a rollercoaster, vilified by your friends but trusted by the teacher. Anyone trying too hard – 'Miss, Miss, pick me, pick me!', waving their hand in the air – was not usually a candidate. Sometimes they chose the good ones, sometimes the rascally ones. Music teachers chose the ones with a modicum of talent and PE teachers always chose the sporty ones!

If you were canny you could use your position to your advantage. Being always smiled upon meant many an indiscretion and misdemeanour would be overlooked, which gave many the scope to get up to untold mischief. As you can imagine my goal in life was to become a dinner lady's pet. This meant more mash, more custard and more tart!

Any dessert that sticks to the roof of your mouth with such soft gooeyness deserves to be as fondly remembered as this pudding. The mere thought of butterscotch tart makes my fillings ache and my tummy rumble. The way the custard slightly melted the butterscotch filling is the stuff of dreams.

🖊 Ingredients

Pastry

250g plain flour

125g butter or margarine

cold water

Filling

170g butter

170g soft brown sugar

35g plain flour

100ml milk

How to...

1. Preheat oven to 200°C/Gas 6.
2. Follow the instructions for pastry given in the Cornflake Tart recipe
3. Roll out the pastry. Line a tin 14 inches by 8 inches. Prick with a fork, fill with baking beans and bake blind for 15 minutes. Allow to cool.
4. Put the milk and butter in a large pan and place over a gentle heat.
5. Once the butter is melted bring the milk and butter mixture to the boil.
6. Add in the sugar to the milk and butter mixture and, once combined, sift in the flour. Using a wooden spoon or balloon whisk beat well until the mixture is smooth and lump free.
7. Simmer gently for 2 or 3 minutes; keep your arms and any small children out of the way as this can be temperamental.
8. Beat again until the mixture becomes a little grainy and lighter in colour. A minute or two should be enough. Leave to cool.
9. When cool, spread into the pastry case and refrigerate until cold. Once cold cut and serve with plenty of hot custard. Do not be tempted to cut this when still warm as there will be a really sticky mess in the kitchen!

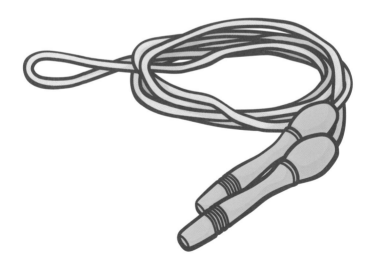

Gypsy tart

You can choose your friends but you can't choose your relatives and when they are at your school this brings with it a whole raft of problems. Comparing you to your sporting sisters and brainy brothers almost always turned out to be a serious let-down for all concerned.

Younger brothers and sisters seriously cramped your style, snitching on you to your parents if you were told off in assembly, threatening to tell if they spotted you having a secret snog and 'innocently' letting slip to your friends about your teddy and blanket at bedtime.

Aunties in school, either real or just your mum's best friend, could help or hinder. Aunts in the office never sent you home just because you 'had a tummy ache'. Aunts in the dinner hall, however, were another matter. They were always good for seconds. As for parents in school, don't even go there...

Here is another close relative, this time to the butterscotch tart, but gypsy tart has a much less sticky texture and a creamier flavour. Such is the sweetness of gypsy tart that it does not need a sweet pastry case. As the trendier restaurants have been championing recently, the slight saltiness of the savoury pastry enhances the sugariness of the tart. That and the fact that school cooks made one batch of pastry and they were not going to put sugar in it in case they needed the leftovers for chicken pie tomorrow.

📝 Ingredients

Pastry

250g plain flour
125g butter or margarine
cold water

Filling

1 large can of evaporated milk, fridge cold
350g soft brown sugar

How to....

1. Preheat the oven to 190°C/Gas 5.
2. Follow the instructions for pastry given in the Cornflake Tart recipe.
3. Roll out the pastry; line a tin 6 inches by 10 inches. Prick with a fork, fill with baking beans and bake blind for 15 minutes. Allow to cool.
4. Take the evaporated milk from the fridge; it must be very cold for this recipe to work properly. Crumble in the soft brown sugar, breaking up any large lumps with your fingers.
5. Using an electric whisk or child labour (your own children, please!), whisk for at least 10 minutes. The sugar will dissolve into the milk and the bubbly mixture will thicken to a caramel colour.
6. Pour into the part-baked pastry shell and place in the oven. Bake for 10 minutes and then turn the oven off and leave the tart in until cold.
7. The filling will set as the temperature drops. Place in the fridge and keep chilled until time to serve. Don't keep this in a warm room before serving as the filling will return to evaporated milk. Not a good look!
8. Book a dental appointment.

Jaffa tart

School puddings made use of what was available: fruit in season, jams and preserves and, most importantly for us, sugar and chocolate. Jaffa tart uses two favourites: oranges and chocolate. Jaffa cakes were seen as a party food in the sixties and seventies and I suppose the school cook saw a fast-moving bandwagon and jumped on it.

Jaffa cakes were a huge treat and so is this pudding. If only school cooks had thought of a way to make a pudding version of iced gems and chocolate fingers my world would have been complete.

I first ate Jaffa tart as a teacher, but failed miserably in my efforts to get the recipe, not because it was a secret but I just didn't get round to asking the cook before she retired. The orangey base was tangy and gooey but didn't have the taste or texture of marmalade. The only filling that comes close is orange curd. It is really very easy to make and you will have some left over to make a second tart or to have on your morning toast.

If you really can't be bothered with the fuss or just don't have time to make the curd then shredless orange marmalade will do as a good substitute.

Ingredients

 Pastry

250g plain flour
125g butter or margarine
cold water

Filling

2 navel oranges
1 lemon, juiced
75g butter
225g sugar
3 eggs, well beaten
100g dark chocolate

How to...

① Preheat oven to 200°C/Gas 6.

② Roll out the pastry; line a tin 14 inches by 8 inches. Prick with a fork, fill with baking beans and bake blind for 15 minutes. Remove the baking beans and bake for a further 5 minutes. Allow to cool.

③ Turn the oven down to 170°C/Gas 4.

④ To make the orange curd, grate the zest from one of the oranges and place in a heatproof bowl. Add the juice from both oranges and the lemon. Add in the sugar, butter and eggs and place the bowl over a pan of barely simmering water.

⑤ Heat gently, whisking all the time until the curd mixture thickens. Leave to cool.

⑥ Once cool spread the pastry case with the orange curd mixture. Any remaining curd mixture can be kept refrigerated for up to a week.

⑦ Grate the chocolate over the orange-curd-filled tart case. Keep refrigerated until needed. Serve with wither warm custard or vey cold cream.

Chocolate and toothpaste tart

Chocolate came in relatively few guises when I was growing up. Apart from the Pink Panther bar which was a strawberry flavoured, bright pink, slightly grainy confection, the choice was was milk, plain or white. If you wanted to buy a chocolate that lasted and would have to be sucked rather than chewed, you purchased a bar from a railway chocolate machine. Railway chocolate was almost impossible to break without a sledgehammer. If you needed that dark 'chocolatey' hit that we know today from very high percentage of cocoa solids then cocoa was the solution.

Cocoa gives chocolate and toothpaste tart its depth of flavour and the milk powder will keep your bones strong too! This was the school cooks' summer answer to chocolate sponge and custard. It was very important to get a chocolate fix and this did it for me. Where does the toothpaste come in you may well ask? Now school cooks were a canny lot and I have heard rumours of some very interesting ingredients in a few of their recipes but toothpaste isn't one of them. It refers to the squirt of mock cream on the top of each square of the chocolate tart.

✎ Ingredients

Pastry
250g plain flour
125g butter or margarine
Cold water

Filling
100g softened butter
100g icing sugar
100g dried milk powder (not granules)
2 tbsp cocoa
2 tbsp hot chocolate
3 tbsp hot water

How to...

1. Preheat oven to 200°C/Gas 6.
2. Follow the instructions for pastry given in the cornflake tart recipe.
3. Roll out the pastry; line a tin 14 inches by 8 inches. Prick with a fork, fill with baking beans and bake blind for 15 minutes. Remove the baking beans and bake for a further 5 minutes. Allow to cool.
4. Turn the oven down to 170°C/Gas 4.
5. Cream together the butter and icing sugar until the mixture becomes very pale.
6. Beat in the milk powder ensuring there are no lumps.
7. Place the cocoa and hot chocolate into a small bowl and mix together with the hot water to make a smooth paste.
8. Add this smooth paste to the creamed butter, sugar and dried milk mixture.
9. Beat this chocolate paste well until any graininess disappears and it becomes glossy.
10. Pour into the cooked and cooled pastry case and refrigerate until set. Pipe swirls of mock cream on to individual portions to maintain the toothpaste element if you feel the need.

Pink slice and cornflakes

Despite trying to get us all to conform, schools were home to many a strange item.

Plimsolls, for example, are a very peculiar and unique form of footwear. Combine the heady mix of excited children, shiny no-grip plimsolls and a highly polished floor and you have a potentially dangerous situation. With stealth, cunning and a deaf ear to the teacher you could pick up enough speed to rival an Olympic downhill skier. Occasionally you met your comeuppance – a stray carrot or dollop of semolina would halt you like a rut on a black run. Worse still was the wet patch of dubious origin occasionally left by the previous class of five-year-olds. Hitting the wet, highly polished floor sped you up and your only way of stopping was to cartwheel into the wall bars. The rest of the lesson would be spent outside the secretary's office or in the medical room with you clutching a witch hazel-soaked wad of cotton wool to your injured body part.

Only in schools could pink slice and cornflakes have been served. No way could this be described as a traditional dessert. Sometimes this was served on a pastry base, but if time was short it wasn't. I am almost certain this may have glowed in the dark and there were the inevitable rumours that this was not made from jelly and milk but blood and other bodily fluids! School was the only place I recall jelly being so solid that it could be cut and served in large cuboids.

✏ *Ingredients*

Pastry

250g plain flour
125g butter or margarine
Cold water

(Or buy a pack of ready made)

Pink mousse

1 pack strawberry jelly
1 small can evaporated milk
(refrigerated)

Cornflake topping

125g caster sugar
125g butter
220g cornflakes
125g golden syrup

How to...

1. Preheat oven to 200°C/Gas 6.

2. Line a rectangular baking tin with pastry and bake blind.

3. Melt jelly into 150ml of boiling water and then add 150ml of cool water. This is now double strength! Do not panic. Place in the fridge until just setting around the edges.

4. Remove the jelly and the evaporated milk from the fridge. Place the milk into a bowl and whisk until frothy. Add in the barely set jelly and whisk again until very bubbly. Pour the pink mousse either on to the pastry base or into a rectangular dish. Place back into the fridge until set, this will not take long.

5. Place the sugar, syrup and butter in a large pan and heat gently until the butter has melted. Give the mixture a good stir and add in the cornflakes a few handfuls at a time until either the cornflakes are all added or the toffee mixture is all used up. Mix well to make sure each cornflake is sticky. I generally test this by having a quick spoonful but be careful as hot sugar burns!

6. Place the cornflake mix on to the mousse and serve immediately.

Apple pie

Adults have a tendency to overcomplicate things. For the most part, however, children much prefer the less complex. PE was a time when teachers might try to introduce us to games with long sets of rules with specially delineated playing areas. But whilst football, netball and cricket played important parts in our lives what we really enjoyed were games such as Traffic Lights which would keep us amused for a long while. Stuck in the Mud and Captain's Coming were hot favourites too.

These games didn't rely on your ability with a ball and could be played in a variety of spaces. There were no such luxuries as having 'lives' or second chances. If you were 'out' you were 'out'. The fear of being 'out' galvanised even the most sluggish of individuals to get moving. French cricket and bench ball did involve ball skills but again the being 'out' concentrated the mind somewhat, as did the vilification from your team when you slunk away to stand by the hall wall. Getting out first meant you would almost certainly be one of the last chosen when the class was divided into teams for the next game.

Fortunately the school cook didn't have time to complicate things. Such a classic dish needs love and attention and apple pie's simplicity is what makes it taste so good. As does the vast quantity of custard you will need to make, as I can guarantee everyone will want seconds.

✏ *Ingredients*

Pastry

250g plain flour
125g butter or margarine
Cold water

Filling

4 large Bramley apples
Splash of water
Knob of butter
Sugar
1 tsp cinnamon or a few
cloves
A handful of raisins

How to...

1. Preheat oven to 200°C/Gas 6.

2. Follow the instructions for pastry given in the cornflake tart recipe. Leave the pastry to rest in the fridge or pop to the shops and buy a pack of ready-made.

3. Peel and core the apples. Cut into generous-sized chunks and place in a saucepan with a splash of water, a knob of butter and sugar to taste.

4. Gently cook the apples until the edges of each piece just begins to soften. Don't cook to a mush as the apples will continue to cook in the oven. Put the part-cooked apples into a baking dish and top with a little more sugar if it tastes very sharp. A little scatter of cinnamon is good too. You could add a few cloves but warn the apple pie eaters that they are lurking under the custard. School cooks also added raisins, probably to boost our fruit levels. Add them if you like.

5. Roll out the pastry and cover the apple mixture. Sprinkle the surface of the pie with caster sugar and make a small slit in the pie crust to let steam escape and bake for 20 to 30 minutes or until the pastry is golden brown and the apple is bubbling.

6. Serve with custard, or ice cream if you have to.

Fruit crumble

Some schools had well-tended gardens. Others had tubs and hanging baskets. Mine had a bare patch of earth with a couple of tussocks of grass and a vast expanse of tarmac.

So my experience of growing things came from the nature table: bowls of shiny mahogany-coloured conkers gave way to holly branches and photographs of snow-covered hill tops. Bowls of daffodils and hyacinths came next to bring fragrance to the classroom. Then along came the tadpoles. As soon as the tadpoles arrived we knew that the wet flannel and cress would be next, accompanied by the jam jar containing blotting paper and a bean seed. Sometimes carrot tops would be encouraged into growth and I once remember an avocado stone impaled with cocktail sticks sitting morosely over a jar of water, stubbornly refusing to sprout.

Other school staff took their gardening much more seriously. If the cook had a plum tree in her garden you knew you would get a plum crumble at least once a fortnight until the glut was over. Crumbles were as seasonal as possible. Chewy and crunchy at the same time, this pudding is heaven on an aluminium spoon. Crumble, beautiful as it is, didn't escape the folklore of the playground. By using red fruits the whole thing could look like an open wound, and adding custard it became infected with pus. Aren't kids just fantastic?

✏ Ingredients

Crumble topping
250g plain flour
125g butter or margarine
125g sugar

Fruit filling
Enough fruit to fill the bottom of a large baking dish
(choose from rhubarb, plum, apricot, apple, pear or
whatever you can scrump!)
Sugar to taste

How to...

1. Preheat oven to 200°C/Gas 6.
2. Cut up the fruit into manageable pieces (with rhubarb about 2cm or 1 inch sticks), halve stone fruit and remove stones, cut apples and pears into good-sized chunks. Lay in the bottom of a deep baking dish. Be generous.
3. Try a small piece of fruit and add sugar to taste. You can liven up this dish with spices if you like. Rhubarb works well with ginger, apples go well with cinnamon and pears love a splash of red wine.
4. Place the flour, butter and sugar into a separate bowl and rub together with your fingers until the mix resembles breadcrumbs.
5. Pour this mixture over the fruit and bake for 30 minutes until the fruit is bubbling away.
6. Leave to stand for a few minutes. The word volcanic is not an exaggeration! Serve with custard.

Semolina pudding

'Have you heard? Tracy has broken her arm.' 'No! How did that happen?' 'Well...' So the tale begins: recounts of trips, falls, pushes and bike accidents. We loved the drama and excitement of it all.

Of course the most gossip was generated if someone broke a limb at school. The playground jungle drums went into meltdown and this was true too for the mums gossiping at the school gate. What began as a broken wrist would be transformed into a full body cast by the time the last child had left school. Fractures meant casts and casts meant instant fame, with it came the chance to indulge in a little one-upmanship. Getting to sign someone's cast showed your social standing in the playground. Where your signature or message could go was telling too: having to sign on the underside of the cast in a place that was often covered with clothing reminded you just how far you still had to climb up that playground social ladder.

If you have ever used plaster of Paris you will know why it makes me think of semolina. Its texture is very similar; also I wonder how many people ended up in a cast having slipped on the stray blob that was always dropped on the floor on semolina days?

My daughter has horrified me by saying she has never had this for lunch. School dinners are not what they used to be! By the time I have perfected this recipe she will have plenty of experience of this pudding, let me tell you.

✏ Ingredients

40g semolina
1 pint full-fat milk
25g sugar
25g butter
Grated nutmeg

How to...

1. Preheat oven to 150°C/Gas 2.

2. Heat the milk and sugar in a pan until warmed. Gently tip in the semolina a little at a time. Stir continuously. We are not trying to re-create this dish with the lumps.

3. Melt in the butter and allow to simmer for 10 minutes. The mixture should thicken by this point.

4. Place in a buttered dish, sprinkle the top of the dish with cinnamon and bake in the oven for 30 to 40 minutes or serve straight from the pan into bowls and add grated chocolate as a garnish.

5. If you bake this dish, serve with jam or syrup or fruit compote.

Stewed prunes

Combining stewed prunes with hard medicated toilet roll was a cruel and unusual punishment. The regularity of the nation was a government obsession and here is their solution for those still in school. The prunes were ladled out on to your plate; depending on who was serving you might get the prunes or the custard first. This caused consternation in the same way that milk or no milk first does with tea drinkers. Me, I preferred prune then custard as it gave me a chance to be surprised when finding a prune in my spoonful of custard. I also wasn't too keen on how the slick of prune juice looked sat on top of the thick yellow custard.

If no one was looking you could fire the stones across the room just by squeezing your fingers together and allowing the stones to slip away at speed. I like the idea of this but really I enjoyed collecting the stones on the edge of my plate.

In the present climate I do not think we would be given any stoned fruit at lunchtime, lest we should choke on the stones. At my school I really don't recall anyone choking but if they did a swift thump between the shoulder blades and a rebuke to eat more slowly and carefully would have been forthcoming from a dinner lady.

When you have finished eating all the prunes tell your fortune by using the fortune-telling rhyme:

Tinker, tailor, soldier, sailor
Rich man, poor man, beggar man, thief
Doctor, lawyer, Indian chief
This year, next year, sometime, never!

 **Ingredients**

150g dried prunes
2 tbsp sugar
Water to cover

How to...

1. Cover the prunes with water and leave overnight to plump up.
2. Add a little more water the following day if needed to cover the prunes and bring slowly to the boil. Stir in the sugar and simmer for 10 minutes.
3. Allow to cool slightly and serve in a rimmed bowl with custard.
4. Place the stones around the edge of the bowl as you finish eating each prune.

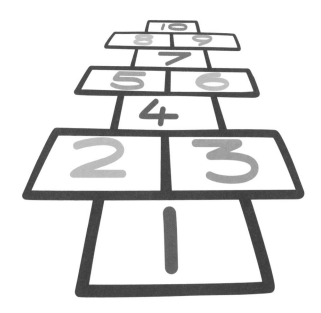

Iced sponge

Every classroom had one. It was screwed to the wall high up behind the teacher's desk. Ours had two silver knobs, one to tune the radio and one to control the volume. Woe betide anyone caught fiddling with those knobs.

In the days before CDs and digital media, if you wanted to listen to a radio programme it was listen live or don't listen at all. The programmes always started at peculiar times like 11.23 am or 2.47pm. With our BBC-published pupils' book, we would sing along to the music programme, each term having a new topic and set of songs to learn. Many of us were familiar with listening to the radio at home, so having stories read in weekly instalments was something we enjoyed. Waiting to find out the result of the previous week's cliff hanger was positively looked forward to. The Iron Man by Ted Hughes is one that sticks firmly in my memory. The radio moved us away from the classics so beloved of our older teachers and proved a simple but effective introduction to modern children's literature.

The simple things are often the best. Soft sponge, crunchy topping and bright pink chemically flavoured custard – what more could a child want? Seconds perhaps?

🖉 Ingredients

175g butter or margarine

175g caster sugar

2 large eggs

225g self-raising flour

2 tablespoons milk

Vanilla extract

125g icing sugar

Water

Hundreds and thousands

How to....

1. Preheat oven to 180°C/Gas 4.
2. Line a rectangular tin with baking parchment.
3. Place butter and sugar in a large bowl and beat together well. Continue creaming until the butter and sugar mixture becomes paler in colour.
4. Beat the eggs in a separate bowl, then add half of this beaten egg into the mixture, and stir it in well. Add in a couple of tablespoons of the flour, then the rest of the egg, and beat again. Now is the time to add in the vanilla extract.
5. Taking a metal spoon, very gently fold in the rest of the flour. Be gentle and use a cutting and folding movement to combine the flour without losing any air from the mix. When all the flour is combined add in a tablespoon of milk.
6. Check the consistency of your cake mix. Gather up a little on a spoon and hold over the bowl. If it drops off then the mixture is ready; if it remains on the spoon you need to add another tablespoon of milk and check again.
7. Put this mix into a 11 inches by 7 inches rectangular cake tin and bake for 30 minutes at 180°C/Gas 4 until firm and golden brown.
8. When cooked, cool for a short while in the tin and then place on a wire rack to get completely cold.
9. Ice with simple water icing and scatter generously with hundreds and thousands. Another version has a red seedless jam topping that then has a scattering of desiccated coconut. You could add coconut to the cake mixture too if you wanted to. Try adding 50g of coconut and leave out 25g of the flour.
10. Serve with pink custard (see Extras for recipe).

Chocolate sponge

Many schools operate a monitor or prefect system, where jobs with very little power and responsibility were shared out amongst the more trustworthy element of the school community. Some tasks came with the opportunity to visit unknown worlds (making the teacher's tea in the staffroom). Others brought the school peacocks the chance to be permanently on show (the hymn-number changers in assemblies).

One monitor position would – as my husband can testify – get you extra chocolate pudding. Sweeping the dinner hall with the caretaker's large broom got you seconds. The boredom of walking up and down, across and back clearing the floor of discarded cabbage and biscuit crumbs was rewarded with more pudding. There were apparently always plenty of volunteers for that job. I suspect even without the food as a reward there are many boys who would have gladly spent time pushing an oversized broom around a very shiny floor, especially if it was one of those brooms that folds into a V shape to help you get into the corners!

Here is a pudding that has a lot to answer for. So many people cite school chocolate pudding as the beginning of their love of all things 'chocolatey'. Served hot with rich chocolate or mint custard this pudding is heavenly.

Ingredients

150g plain flour

50g cocoa

100g golden syrup

100g soft brown sugar

100g butter

5ml milk

1 egg

1? level tsp bicarbonate of soda

How to...

1. Preheat the oven to 190°C/Gas 5.
2. Line a rectangular tin 8 inches by 12 inches with baking parchment.
3. Sift flour and cocoa together into a large mixing bowl.
4. Measure out the golden syrup and pour into a saucepan, add the brown sugar and margarine, and using a wooden spoon stir the mixture over a gentle heat until the margarine has melted. Remove from the heat and allow to cool slightly.
5. Add the milk to the liquids then beat the egg. Stir the bicarbonate of soda and egg mixture into the milk, syrup, sugar and butter.
6. Stir all these ingredients into the sifted flour and cocoa, beating well to make sure the mixture is smooth.
7. Pour the mixture into an 8 by 12 inch tin and bake the cake in oven for 20 to 25 minutes. Turn out the cake on to a wire tray to cool slightly. Once cooled cut into generous squares.
8. Serve with chocolate or mint custard (see Extras for recipes).

Pineapple
upside-down cake

I loved being upside down.

Handstands should have given me ample opportunity to be upside down, but they weren't enough. Somewhere on most school grounds there was a metal handrail that called out to be swung on and rolled around. If someone else had got to the bars first there was often a tree branch or a school fence that could be used to support our views of an upside-down world.

Hanging on by just your knees with your hands waving at your friends is one of the most carefree feelings I can remember. Turning upside down after pineapple upside-down cake was not always a good idea. What you really needed to do was sit still and let it all go down. We didn't of course and the sticky sweetness of this cake gave us huge amounts of energy that needed to be run off.

For us pineapple upside-down cake was exotic and exciting with a much-loved sticky coating. Glacé cherry lovers chose their seats carefully. Nestling between several cherry haters could gain you up to half a dozen extra red jewels on your plate. Taking the time to eat around the pineapple ring, saving the juice-drenched sponge underneath, was bliss.

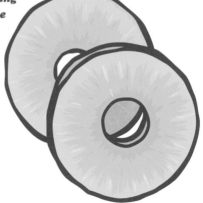

🖊 *Ingredients*

3 eggs weighed in their shells
An equivalent weight of caster sugar
An equivalent weight of self-raising flour
An equivalent weight of butter or margarine
1 tbsp pineapple juice
1 can pineapple rings
3 glacé cherries, halved
2 tbsp soft brown sugar
Vanilla extract

How to...

1. Heat the oven to 190°C/Gas 5.
2. Line a rectangular tin 6 inches by 10 inches with baking parchment to prevent the pineapples and sugar from welding themselves to the tin.
3. Drain the pineapple rings and reserve 1 tbsp of juice.
4. Sprinkle the brown sugar on to the parchment and lay out the pineapple rings evenly. Adorn the centre of each ring with half a glacé cherry cut side up for the best aesthetics.
5. Weigh the eggs in their shells; now weigh out an equal weight to the eggs of sugar, butter and self-raising flour.
6. Cream together the butter and sugar until the mixture becomes paler in colour and lighter in texture.
7. Beat in the eggs one at a time. If the mixture starts to look a little grainy add a spoonful of the weighed-out flour.
8. Fold in the remaining flour carefully. Slacken the mixture with 1 tbsp of the reserved pineapple juice and a 1/2 tsp of vanilla extract.
9. Spoon the mixture into the tin evenly and smooth out, trying not to disturb the cherries.
10. Bake for 30 to 35 minutes or until golden and well risen. Leave to cool in the tin for 5 minutes. Turn out and carefully peel back the paper to reveal the cake in all its golden and glistening glory.

Rice or tapioca pudding

Learning to do a handstand was a rite of passage. Showing your knickers didn't cross your mind as everyone's looked the same; you just needed to remember to tuck your vest in. Playgrounds the country over were filled with upside-down girls. We had synchronised handstands, group handstands and even endurance handstands: perhaps we should have made it an Olympic sport - we'd have won all the medals.

Woe betide anyone who got too close to the handstand area – yes it existed, as the length of time your wrists could support a handstand varied. When you had to return to the upright world there was no waiting and if someone was walking past you had no option but to kick them in the ear. Of course this was never done on purpose; at least that's what you told the dinner lady.

Earlier in this book I confessed to being a lover of milk puddings. The creaminess and the warmth were so lovely. Whilst I preferred the texture of rice to tapioca, I was more than happy to eat either. What really made it for me though was the swirl of rose hip syrup or blob of jam. I was never a stirrer of puddings. I always ate around the sweet jammy dollop and slowly savoured it long after my friends had left to do handstands up the playground wall.

✏️ Ingredients

50g pudding rice or tapioca

1 pint full-fat milk

25g sugar

25g butter

Grated nutmeg

How to...

1. Preheat oven to 150°C/Gas 2.
2. Wash the rice. (Don't do this to the tapioca or you will quickly find why it was nicknamed frog spawn!) Place in a buttered gratin-type dish.
3. Pour over the milk and stir in the sugar. Place in the oven and stir every 15 minutes for the first hour.
4. Grate a little fresh nutmeg over the surface of the pudding and place back in the oven for the final hour's cooking until the surface is golden.
5. Serve with rose hip syrup or a dollop of jam.

Ginger cake and lemon sauce

With everyone told to wear the same clothes, how could children be told apart? Very simple: check our collars and read our names. Some parents wrote in names with biro. This was fine until the first wash. It might not shift ketchup, but washing powder could remove ball-point pen instantly. Friends were reduced to sniffing unnamed jumpers to see which one smelt of home. Sniffing nameless hockey socks wasn't an issue for me. Late August evenings in our house were spent sewing in woven name tapes. You might have thought we would all find this conformity stifling. Not a bit of it. When allowed the freedom to choose we opted to wear the same shoes, had the same school bags and even wore our socks in the same peculiar way.

Ginger cake and lemon sauce, by contrast, was a very unique pudding; no element of it crossed over into another dish. Always served with lemon sauce this was a dish for the sophisticated palate. The lemon sauce was not always appreciated as the clear liquid had the look, but thankfully not the taste, of thick bleach! At least it made a change from custard.

✐ Ingredients

Ginger cake
100g butter or margarine
150g dark muscovado or
molasses sugar
1 large egg
300g self-raising flour
125ml milk
2 tbsp golden syrup
(use treacle if you want an
even deeper flavour)
1 tsp ground ginger
½ tsp freshly ground
black pepper

Lemon sauce
170g caster sugar
2 tbsp cornflour
300ml water
3 tbsp lemon juice
Rind of 1 lemon
2 tsp butter

How to...

1. Heat the oven to 180°C/Gas 4.
2. Line a tin 11 inches by 7 inches with baking parchment.
3. Place butter and sugar in a large bowl and beat together well. Continue creaming until the butter and sugar mixture becomes paler in colour.
4. Sieve together the ginger and flour and add the black pepper.
5. Beat the egg in a separate bowl and add half of this beaten egg to the mixture, then stir in well. Add in a couple of tablespoons of the dry ingredients then the rest of the egg and beat again. Now is the time to add in the syrup or treacle.
6. Taking a metal spoon very gently fold in the rest of the flour. Be gentle and use a cutting and folding movement to combine the flour without losing any air from the mix. When all the flour is combined add half of the milk.
7. Check the consistency of your cake mix. Gather up a little on a spoon and hold over the bowl. If it drops off then the mixture is ready; if it remains on the spoon you need to add another tablespoon of milk and check again.
8. Put this mix into the cake tin and bake for 40 minutes until firm and golden brown.
9. When cooked, cool for a short while in the tin and then place on a wire rack to get completely cold.
10. To make the lemon sauce combine together the sugar and the cornflour, add a little of the water to make a paste and than add in the remaining water. Bring to the boil and simmer until thickened.
11. Once this is about as thick as double cream add in the lemon juice, rind and butter. Combine well and pour over the ginger cake whilst both are still warm.

Doughnuts

Birthday parties were such fun. Standing in the queue at the post office to buy a six pack of invitations was the start of the excitement. Who to ask and who to leave out was traumatic but necessary. You could only get a certain number of children around your dining-room table at home and your mum wasn't going to set up the picnic table as well. Planning the games was easy: you had to play pass the parcel, hunt the thimble and Kim's game.

Party dresses were made and matching ribbons were tied into plaits and ponytails. Some mums very ambitiously transformed chocolate Swiss roll into trains and made houses from gingerbread and sweets. Other mums made a ballerina cake with sponge skirt and a Sindy doll stuck in the top. To be honest, we didn't care what it looked like just as long as we had a slice to take home wrapped in a serviette. What we liked best were the cakes and biscuits. Nibbling the tops off iced gems immediately transports me back to cake and candle heaven.

It seems completely unbelievable these days that schools served children fried and sugared balls of dough for pudding, but they did. To compound this crime, in my school it was often partnered with caffeine in the form of milky coffee. So many happy lunch hours were passed trying to eat a doughnut without licking your lips. We all knew this was an impossible task but were thankful for the opportunity to have a go.

Ingredients

250g plain flour

2 tsp baking powder

Knob of butter

1 tsp salt

110g sugar

125ml milk

1 egg beaten

Oil for frying

Additional caster sugar to dust

Jam to fill if required

How to...

1. In a bowl mix together the dry ingredients. Add in the knob of butter and rub this in until it resembles fine breadcrumbs.
2. Stir in the egg and enough milk to make a soft but not too sticky dough. You may not need all the 125ml of milk.
3. Well flour a board and tip the dough on to this. Flour the top of the dough and either push or roll out until the dough is 2 cm (approx 3/4 inch) thick.
4. For ring doughnuts: using a cutter cut out rounds and using a smaller cutter cut the hole in the middle of the doughnut.
5. For jam doughnuts: using a large round cutter cut out rounds. Place a spoonful of jam in the middle and pinch the top of the doughnut closed leaving you with a ball shape. Roll in your hands to really close the dough.
6. Heat a frying pan containing 2cm (approx 3/4 inch) depth of vegetable oil. Fry the doughnuts gently on all sides until golden brown. Drain on kitchen paper and when drained toss in a little more sugar to coat.
7. Sit with friends and family and try to eat a whole doughnut without licking your lips.

Swedish tea ring

Everyone organised themselves into little groups at school. Cliques formed around music, make-up and occasionally geekiness. Each clique had its own rules and codes.

Our clique had several weekly rituals. My favourite one revolved around the fact that everyone else's life was significantly more exciting than mine. As soon as the paper boy dropped the new copy of Jackie through the door it was taken to school. The articles were read, the make-up tips and clothing features were discussed and the problem of which poster to take off your bedroom wall so you could put up this week's pin-up was mulled over. The best was saved until last: the problem page. Oh, how we wished we were the ones plagued by the readers' problems. Wouldn't it be great to have two boys wanting to kiss you at the youth club disco? How awful that the boy hadn't paid for her bus fare – of course she should dump him! No one ever wanted to admit that, like the girl in the magazine, they fancied their friend's brother but we all secretly did.

Happily for us the arrival of the magazine often coincided with Swedish tea ring for pudding. Seriously sophisticated and grown-up fare, at least that's what we thought, as we ate this iced cinnamon spiced bun and drank the milky coffee that went along with it. In our minds we were transformed from spotty 13-year-olds into louche philosophers discussing the important questions of the moment. David Cassidy or Donny Osmond – is it possible to like both?

✐ Ingredients

Dough

650g strong white bread flour

60g caster sugar

75g white vegetable fat or lard

1 egg, beaten

1 tsp salt

180ml warm milk

150ml warm water

1 sachet yeast

Filling

50g softened butter
50g caster sugar
50g soft brown sugar
3 tsp ground cinnamon

Topping

150g icing sugar
Enough water to create a stiff
paste

How to...

1. Preheat oven to 190°C/Gas 5 .

2. Place the warm water in a jug and stir in a sprinkle of sugar and the yeast. Keep at a constant room temperature, out of any draughts until the yeast has doubled in size.

3. Sieve the flour into a large bowl and stir in the sugar and salt. Cut the lard or vegetable shortening into the flour and rub in until the vegetable fat resembles breadcrumbs.

4. Pour in the warm milk and stir to begin to incorporate, now add the beaten egg and the yeast mixture. Using a round-bladed knife mix until the dough comes together.

5. Using your hands knead the dough gently but effectively for 5 minutes or so until the dough becomes smooth and silky. If the dough is very soft and 'loose' you may need more flour on your work surface as you work it.

6. Make the dough into a ball and place in an oiled bowl. Cover with a damp cloth. Leave for an hour and a half until well risen.

7. Knock back (punch the dough in the middle to deflate it) and let it rise again for another 45 minutes.

8. On a lightly floured surface roll the dough out to approximately 30cm by 20cm (or 8 inches by 12 inches).

9. In a small bowl beat together the butter, caster sugar, brown sugar and the cinnamon. Spread this over the dough and roll up the dough lengthwise. Place seam side down and join the ends to make a ring.

10. Taking a sharp knife, make cuts every 2cm or roughly every inch. Cut three-quarters of the way through the ring and twist each cut to expose the butter mixture.

11. Leave to rise again for 30 minutes and then bake for 25 to 30 minutes.

12. Once cool but still warm ice with the icing mixture and serve slices with milky coffee and a copy of *Smash Hits*.

Pears and chocolate sauce

On the desk stood two large wooden blocks. One had 36 holes set out in a 6 x 6 pattern drilled into the surface. Each hole housed a school pencil, point upwards and freshly sharpened. Next to this sat a rack of 18 scissors, point down and ready to cut. These two items let us know that we would be having Art today.

Working on your latest masterpiece always made the time fly by. As the smells wafted in from the dinner hall the anxiety in the classroom would increase. Not only were we all desperate to get to lunch, we were watching those two wooded blocks like hawks. We all knew no one would be allowed to go until every pencil and pair of scissors was accounted for. Each bin was checked, pockets felt and tables crawled under until someone said those magic words, 'Here it is!' Chairs would be tucked in and we would be dismissed table by table to go to lunch.

Making use of seasonal fruit and vegetables was often what the school cook did best, but sometimes they had to use tinned fruit. Don't forget that tinned fruit was seen as a treat, as was the chocolate sauce that goes with it! This was not a day to be kept in at lunchtime. When you got to the canteen all that would be left of the pears was sticky syrup in a bowl and the only chocolate sauce to be seen decorated the chins of luckier children.

✑ Ingredients

Tin of pear halves or quarters (you can poach your own too)

1 bar good dark chocolate

300 ml double cream (or gold top milk)

1 tbsp golden syrup

How to...

1. Open the pears and drain off the juice or syrup.
2. In a heat-proof bowl over barely simmering water melt the chocolate and syrup together. Do not allow the chocolate to get too hot or it will seize and become grainy.
3. Once melted together add the cream or milk and stir until thoroughly mixed.
4. Serve two halves or several quarters of the pear in a bowl and pour over the chocolate sauce.
5. If no one is looking, lick the bowl.

☀ Variations

Pears were also served with chocolate custard and occasionally the sticky chocolate syrup used for making cornflake cakes. Please make whichever was used at your school.

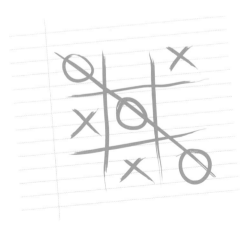

Macaroni pudding

New foods in the sixties and seventies seemed to embrace changes in technology and a move towards the space age. Imagining ourselves to be astronauts we were excited by the thought of instant food rehydration, but usually the potato, meat and always the onions failed to reconstitute fully, leaving you to chew for ages, give up and then have the food expand inside you with severe gastric consequences.

More successful were the foods placed in tubes ready to be squeezed out onto crackers or straight into your mouth if mum wasn't looking. It might only have been shrimp-flavoured cheese but we thought we were Buzz Aldrin as we layered the spread on a Ritz cracker. If a food could be manufactured entirely out of chemicals we hailed it as miraculous. Those butterscotch Instant Whips spring to mind as something only a chemist could love. Tinned food was still king of the pantry but snapping close at its heels were the pretenders, boil in the bag food and frozen. I have vague memories of macaroni coming out of a tin at my Nan's house but a friend tells me she had this for pudding at her school. That is what is so great about nostalgia: everyone remembers something different. As a connoisseur of milk puddings I wish I had had the chance to try this earlier.

🖉 Ingredients

50g macaroni (not quick cook!)

1 pint milk

25g sugar

1 egg, beaten

Butter

How to...

1. Preheat oven to 160°C/Gas 3.
2. Place the milk into a pan and cook over a low heat.
3. Break the macaroni into the milk and slowly bring to simmering point.
4. Simmer gently for 30 minutes. At this stage you must watch the pan like a hawk. If it boils over you will have a really miserable time cleaning the hob and the kitchen will smell vile.
5. Allow to cool slightly and stir in the well-beaten egg. Place the cooked macaroni and egg mixture into a buttered dish, add the sugar and bake for 30 minutes until lightly browned and crusty.
6. Serve with stewed fruit or a dollop of jam.

Bananas and custard

Long before the National Curriculum and league tables, the sole job of a teacher was to fill your head with facts and train your hands for skills. No one really checked to see if these facts were particularly useful or relevant as long as your head was chock full of them and you could if required regurgitate them under examination conditions. I can decline Latin words, draw maps to show the positions of British coal deposits (circa 1979) and explain the action of osmosis clearly and concisely. This is all very worthy, but not very useful unless of course you intend on making your living from cable TV quiz shows.

Another fact told to me as the absolute truth is that bananas are not fruits at all but are in fact herbs. Coming with its own wrapper it has long been the staple of packed lunches and fruit bowls. Hot bananas and custard slipped down very easily. Cold and sprinkled with chocolate vermicelli was pretty good too and a very frugal use of the previous days leftovers.

Their versatility didn't end there: put one in a bag with your unripe tomatoes and it will ripen those too – another one of those facts I have always wanted to pass on but have never had the chance until now.

This is not the time for a crème anglaise flavoured by a vanilla pod. Brightly coloured yellow custard made with custard powder gives the full-on retro effect.

✐ Ingredients

Custard powder

1 pint milk

Sugar

Bananas – 1 per person

Chocolate vermicelli (hundreds and thousands) or chocolate shavings

How to...

① Follow the instructions on your tin of custard powder to make a pint of custard. Leave to cool slightly. If this really is too taxing then please buy a carton of ready made custard, snip off the corner of the tetrapak and heat.

② Peel and slice your banana into a bowl. Add in as much custard as you fancy. Leave for a little while to let the bananas warm through. Sit back, enjoy and pretend to be six again.

③ If, and this is a really slim chance, there is any left over then place it in the fridge for tomorrow. Remove from the fridge about 30 minutes before serving and sprinkle with chocolate hundreds and thousands or chocolate shavings.

④ Leftover butterscotch sauce works well too as an extra layer between the bananas and the custard. Hot or cold, I'm not fussy in this case.

Raspberry buns

String had an almost talismanic quality. Pieces of string were saved and wrapped around fingers by grandparents and then left in a drawer to be forgotten. Soap at Christmas came in a variety of humorous shapes and dangled on a thick rope from the tap in the bathroom until it got too wet and fell off into the bath.

Almost every child had a marionette puppet. Given as a birthday or Christmas present they managed approximately five minutes of play value before becoming so incredibly tangled you had to wait until an adult could help untie the knots. Sadly, complete restringing was sometimes the only option open to us but as the puppet didn't come with instructions for this and the illustration on the box was only a representation, most puppets ended up with one leg shorter than the other and a head tilted permanently to one side.

Looking like little volcanoes these luscious raspberry jam buns had the same ability to retain heat as molten lava. Many a mouth was burned due to consumption of one of these whole. Sitting on a pool of custard they looked like a miniature Tracy Island awaiting the arrival of International Rescue. Of course they never came, but we lived in hope. Virgil was my favourite, what a pity he was only a puppet!

✏ Ingredients

100g self-raising flour

pinch salt

50g caster sugar

50g cold butter

1 egg

1 tbs milk if necessary

Jam (red for the volcano effect)

Vanilla extract

How to...

1. Preheat the oven to 225°C/Gas 8.
2. Sift flour into a roomy bowl and then add the salt.
3. Cut the cold butter into flour and using the tips of your fingers rub into the flour until the mixture resembles breadcrumbs.
4. Add in the sugar and stir to combine.
5. In a separate bowl whisk the egg lightly to break it up and stir in the vanilla extract.
6. Pour the egg mixture into the flour, butter, sugar and salt and beat with a wooden spoon. The dough mixture should be stiff enough to handle and retain its shape. Think playdough for grown-ups.
7. The dough should be pliable and not crumbly. If it is crumbly add milk a few drops at a time until the dough becomes silky and smooth. The size of the egg and the type of flour may affect the dough so you may or may not need this milk.
8. Divide the dough into nine equal portions. Roll each portion into a ball and place on a lightly greased baking tray. Using your finger, or the end of a wooden spoon if you have to, make a well in each ball. Fill each well with the jam and pinch the edges together over the top to hold the jam in but not to obscure it completely.
9. Bake for 15 minutes. When cooked cool on a wire rack. I am not joking about the searing volcanic lava heat of hot jam . Try really hard to allow these buns to cool to room temperature before consuming.
10. Pop in a bowl, surround with custard and dream of Virgil, Alan, Brains or Lady Penelope coming to your rescue.

Iced fingers

The words 'fancy dress' filled my mother with dread. Every school fair, village fête and national celebration featured a fancy-dress competition. Usually judged by a local dignitary, the winner was guaranteed a feature and photograph on the front cover of the local paper.

Your chances of winning were entirely dependent on your parents' ability to create a masterpiece from crepe paper and cardboard. Often themed, you could also win if your idea was witty and original. Royal occasions brought out the most patriotic of fancy dress.

Iced buns came with a few variations, mostly on the icing front, usually white, occasionally pink and rarely, but always longed for, chocolate. I have a vague memory of there being red, white and blue buns at school for the Queen's Silver Jubilee in 1977. I am sure that such extravagance only happened the once. Another dilemma dish for me I'm afraid. Should I lick off the icing first, eat the bun and have the icing last or just stuff the whole lot in and be done with it? Usually I went for the latter as it was too tempting to have the bun looking at me as I tried to make a decision.

✐ Ingredients

Dough

650g strong white bread flour
60g caster sugar
75g white vegetable fat or lard
1 egg, beaten
1 tsp salt
180ml warm milk
150ml warm water
1 sachet yeast
Flavourless oil for greasing trays

Topping

150g icing sugar
Enough water to create a stiff paste
Pink and blue food colouring or cocoa powder to create the various hues

How to...

① Preheat oven to 190°C/Gas 5 .

② Place the warm water in a jug and stir in a sprinkle of sugar and the yeast. Leave out of any draughts until the yeast has doubled in size.

③ Into a large bowl sieve the flour and stir in the sugar and salt. Cut the vegetable shortening into the flour and rub in until the vegetable fat resembles breadcrumbs.

④ Pour in the warm milk and stir to begin to incorporate, now add the beaten egg and the yeast mixture. Using a round-bladed knife mix until the dough comes together.

⑤ Using your hands knead the dough gently but effectively for 5 minutes or so until the dough becomes smooth and silky. The dough is very soft and 'loose' so you may need more flour on your work surface as you work it.

⑥ Make the dough into a ball and place in an oiled bowl. Cover with a damp cloth. Leave for an hour and a half until well risen.

⑦ Knock back (punch the dough in the middle to deflate it) and let it rise again for another 45 minutes.

⑧ On a lightly floured surface divide the mixture into cricket ball sized pieces. Roll out into a sausage shape and place on an oiled baking tray to rise again for another 15 minutes.

⑨ Bake in the oven for 15 minutes and leave to cool. When cool ice with your coloured icing of choice. School cooks uses a 1 inch paint brush for this as they were working with large quantities but you can use a spoon.

⑩ If you do use a brush buy a new one!

Treacle tart

'Fur coat and no knickers', 'mutton dressed as lamb' and occasionally, especially after they'd had a sherry, 'tart'. These were phrases that many grandparents used to describe ladies we knew in the local area. For us little girls these women dressed in the most wonderful way. Big wraparound fur coats with blousy over the top dresses and far too much make-up and perfume. High heels and lots of male friends with big cars served to enhance the myths surrounding them. These ladies were despised and envied with about equal measure. No one actually asked how they managed to live without nine-to-five jobs, but assumptions were made. I can't look at a pair of patent shoes without hearing an elderly relative reminding me that if I wore those shoes others would be able to see the colour of my underwear! Quite obviously she didn't she realise that may have been my reason for choosing them in the first place.

Every tart knows that to be successful you need to find a balance between cloying sweetness and acerbic sourness and treacle tart does that every time. Delightfully chewy and such a good way to soak up the custard served with it. The faintest whiff of lemon probably went straight over our heads as youngsters but it is what makes treacle tart the pudding it is now.

🖋 Ingredients

Pastry
250g plain flour
125g butter or margarine
Cold water

Filling
200g golden syrup
25g butter
50g breadcrumbs
Juice of half a lemon
Grated rind of half a lemon

How to...

1. Preheat the oven to 200°C/Gas 6.
2. Line a small cake pan 6 inches by 6 inches with pastry. You can use a small pie dish if you wish.
3. Treacle tarts often came with a lattice top, so if you feel like gilding the lily then re-roll the pastry trimmings and cut into 1 inch wide strips.
4. Warm the syrup and the butter together in a pan gently. Add in the breadcrumbs, lemon zest and juice and stir to combine.
5. Pour the syrup sludge into the pastry and use the strips to form a lattice. I have had them with twisted lattices, very complex woven lattices and I believe you can even buy a special roller to cut the pastry lattice for you. Please do as you see fit.
6. Tidy the pie edges and bake for 30 minutes. Eat with thick custard.

We might not have had tea at school, but we certainly had the biscuits. For some reason every pudding had to have a textural element to it. Often this came in the form of a crumble topping or a pastry case.

But if this wasn't possible, perhaps where boundaries were being pushed and we children were being offered yogurt, then a biscuit gave us something to chew on and more importantly fill us up. Originally designed as a pudding accompaniment, they quickly transformed themselves into the main attraction.

Shortbreads and flapjacks were the staples of family teas and were familiar to us all. Melting moments, refrigerator biscuits and oaty crunch reminded us of the shop bought ones in the tins at home. Treats came in the form of individual Smartie-topped cornflake cakes and crumbly chocolate biscuit cake. Unique to school were the chewy bars of coconut crisp and chocolate cracknel.

The most famous of these school biscuits has to be 'chocolate concrete'. Chocolate concrete's unyielding nature, not to mention the ability to bend spoons more effectively than Uri Geller, is what gave chocolate concrete its name. What a pity today's children are denied the full day-glo experience of fluorescent green mint custard that used to accompany this culinary masterpiece. Why not make some for tea and surprise them?

If the recipes here give a specific tray size then cut the biscuits into the sizes you require. Other recipes make between 12 and 18 biscuits depending on your generosity!

Biscuits

Chocolate concrete

If you wore a school tie by the end of the week it was bound to be decorated by some part of that week's school dinners. So much of the menu had a splash factor. Custard, gravy, beans, tinned tomato juice and even stewed fruit.

How you wore your tie could save you from some of this additional decoration. Some schools wore their ties very short and fat; others tied them back to front to give a very skinny tie. In some schools labels were cut off or ties were chopped as an initiation. Ties denoted your house, your age or even your sporting prowess.

Custard is no respecter of status: it is as happy to stick to a prefect's tie as to first formers. The pudding that caused most custard events was chocolate concrete. Its density was such that chipping away at the custard softened edges was the only way to get a mouthful of food, but this led to blobs of custard shooting around all over the place.

In the days before hyperactivity chocolate concrete was often served with strawberry pink or mint green custard. This variation on shortbread was later served in more progressive establishments with a new fangled dessert called yoghurt.

✐ Ingredients

250g plain flour

125g caster sugar

125g butter or margarine (melted)

60g cocoa

Water

How to...

1. Preheat oven to 180°C/Gas 4.
2. Sift the flour and cocoa into a large mixing bowl. Add the sugar and mix well to combine.
3. Put the butter into a small pan and place over a low flame to melt.
4. Add the melted butter to the dry mixture and stir until the dough comes together into largish clumps. You may need to use your hands. This does not make a ball of dough, more like very uneven breadcrumbs.
5. Pour these into a 12 inch by 7 inch tin and press down using the back of a large metal spoon. Smooth as you press. The surface should appear shiny. Using a pastry brush wet the surface of the biscuit mix. Don't flood it, a gentle caress is enough!
6. Put into the oven for 35 minutes. When cooked, cool for 5 minutes before marking the surface of the biscuits into portions because, as the name suggests, you won't be able to do this once the concrete has set.
7. When completely cool sprinkle the surface with caster sugar. Cut and serve.
8. Pink or green custard is optional, especially if you have children who may need to sleep in the near future.

☀ *Variations*

Substitute plain flour for cocoa and use vanilla sugar for plain concrete.

Shortbread

Crazes are part and parcel of school life. They start slowly and then one weekend everyone gets their pocket money and descends on the local shop, only to find it has sold out of the item in question. I don't remember pester power being quite so prevalent when I needed clackers or a yo-yo but I do remember feeling very left out that we had Co-op milk and only the Unigate milkman gave away Humphrey straws and stickers. Needless to say my mum wasn't changing her milkman just so that I could get a sheet of stickers.

Following trends was something we all did in the playground, but it was not something you expected of the school cook. Yogurt, however, was very trendy and we were at the cutting edge eating pink yogurt and a shortbread round for pudding.

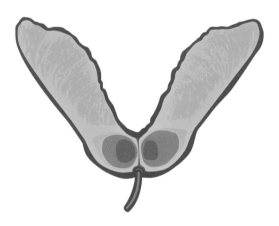

📎 *Ingredients*

150g plain flour
100g butter (soft)
50g caster sugar
1 tbsp granulated sugar for coating

How to...

1. Preheat oven to 190°C/Gas 6.

2. Using a wooden spoon cream together the butter and caster sugar until well combined.

3. Sift in the flour and continue to mix until this is combined also. You may need to use your hands to encourage the last little bit of flour to mix in. This dough will be very soft and pliable.

4. Take a piece of cling film about the size of an A4 piece of paper and lay it on the work surface.

5. Shape the dough into a sausage shape with a diameter of about 4cm. Place the dough on to the sheet of cling film and roll up tightly.

6. Refrigerate for about half an hour at least.

7. Place the granulated sugar on to a chopping board and spread out a little. Remove the dough from the fridge and roll in the granulated sugar. Slice the dough roll into 1cm thick slices. Place on baking trays and bake for 20 minutes. Remove from trays when baked and cool on wire racks.

8. Spoon large dollops of yogurt into a bowl and serve with a cooled crisp biscuit. These biscuits will keep for a day or two in an airtight tin but why bother? Share these with as many people as possible.

Melting moments

School halls seemed gigantic as a small child; the parquet floor twinkled, shone and was waxed to within a fraction of its life daily. The floor finish was seen as a mark of a caretaker's ability: they were able to transform an end of day scuffed hall floor, complete with muddy footprints and smelling of cabbage, into a sparkly, glacially shiny area.

This polishing always had an audience of small boys as ever fascinated by powerful machines. Many asked for a go, but their request would always be met with the universal first response of caretakers the country over – a violent sucking of air over the teeth followed by, 'Bugger off son, I'm busy'. This abrupt rebuttal may well have been brought about because deep in his heart a caretaker knew no one in the school really cared about the depth of the sheen or the symmetry of the buffing circles on the floor. What the teachers wanted was an aroma better than that of sweaty plimsoll, and what the children wanted was not to sit on yesterday's custard. Dropping food on the floor broke the caretaker's heart.

I remember biting into Melting Moments and trying really hard not to drop any bits for the caretaker to clean up. The dinner ladies always had a thing about tidiness but this was much less frightening than the thought of missing out on even the tiniest morsel of these light as air biscuits.

Ingredients

200g plain flour

150g butter or margarine (at room temperature)

80g icing sugar

How to...

1. Preheat oven to 180°C/Gas 4.
2. In a large bowl cream the sifted icing sugar and butter together. Beat until the colour changes to a very pale cream.
3. Sieve in the flour and mix well. Continue beating until the paste is of piping consistency.
4. Pipe either as stars or fingers on to baking trays.
5. If the cook was feeling very extravagant she would top with a slither of glacé cherry and you can do the same.
6. Bake for 10 minutes. Remove from trays and place on cooling racks.
7. Serve with strawberry yogurt.

✳ Variations

Replace 25g of flour with 25g of cocoa for chocolate melting moments or dip the finished biscuits into melted chocolate for real extravagance. A school cook would always use chocolate-flavoured cake covering for this embellishment but I leave the choice of chocolate quality up to you.

Refrigerator biscuits

Schools thrive on systems and organisation. Who has the hall on Tuesday after play? Will the meeting room be free on Wednesday for a PTA meeting? Week in, week out, for children the timetable rolls on. We felt like hamsters on a wheel, Monday we got on and Friday we got off. And it probably wasn't only us: teachers, I am certain, felt exactly the same way about Mondays as I did.

We did, however, all have Friday afternoons. Looked forward to by all it was a relaxed and freer session. This was an opportunity for 'finishing off' and 'choosing time'. Away went the books and out came the colouring, puzzles and the train set. At the far end of the room sat the teacher catching up on her marking with a large cup of coffee and a smile on her face.

That Friday feeling must have affected school cooks too. I seem to remember refrigerator biscuits coming out with stewed fruit or cold custard. When the main course was complicated or the cook was tired at the end of the week these refrigerator biscuits kept the wolf from the door.

✐ Ingredients

200g plain flour
1tsp baking powder
100g butter or margarine (fridge cold)
150g caster sugar
1 egg, beaten

How to...

1. Preheat oven to 180°C/Gas 4.
2. Place the dry ingredients into a bowl and mix well.
3. Cut the butter into the dry ingredients and rub in until the mixture resembles fine breadcrumbs.
4. Using a blunt knife mix in the egg. As the mix begins to come together use your hands to make one ball of dough.
5. Shape the dough into a sausage shape with a diameter of about 4cm. Place the dough on to a sheet of cling film and roll up tightly.
6. Refrigerate for at least four hours, or overnight if possible.
7. Remove from the fridge and slice. Place on baking trays and bake for 10 minutes. Remove from trays when baked and cool on wire racks.

※ Variations

You can make a wide variety of biscuits from this basic recipe. Some suggestions are adding vanilla extract, grated chocolate, dessicated coconut or orange rind. Let your imagination run wild!

Flapjacks

As the space age came to a close there was a surge in peculiar diets: the pineapple diet, the cabbage-soup diet and, most feared, the high-fibre diet. No one wanted to admit their family was on that particular diet but it soon became very obvious to your closest friends. Assemblies all over the country were punctuated by involuntary sounds. Famed amongst many, however, were those who could fart on cue. Interrupting the head teacher's latest rant always brought the house down.

In the days before high-fibre muesli bars and low-GI biscuits flapjacks kept us regular and feeling full until home time. If they had known how good they were for us perhaps we would have had flapjacks more often, but they just made them because they tasted nice. What better reason could there be?

Ingredients

150g rolled oats
75g butter or margarine (melted)
25g soft brown sugar
100g golden syrup

How to...

1. Preheat the oven to 180°C/Gas 4.
2. Melt the sugar, syrup and butter together in a large pan. Cook out for a minute or so until the sugar is dissolved into the syrup and butter mixture.
3. Remove from the heat and stir in the oats.
4. Tip the oaty mixture into a 15cm by 20cm baking tray.
5. Press into the tray using the back of a spoon. Do not use your fingers even if they are asbestos as hot sugar burns. I have scars to prove it.
6. Bake for 25 minutes.
7. When still hot cut into fingers and when cool remove from the tin.
8. Serve with stewed apple, fruit compotes or ice cream.

Chocolate cracknel

Much as I loved chocolate, I also loved toffee. To be fair I have yet to meet a sweetie I absolutely detest. There were one or two, like the Pontefract cake or the Fisherman's Friend, that seemed a little too medicinal but if that was all I could find, covered in fluff in the corner of my coat pocket, then it would still get eaten.

Spangles cut the roof of my mouth and had a curiously gritty texture but I would regularly buy the Old English ones. Two ounces of Tom Thumb drops would last for ages if you ate them one at a time. If you left them in a coat pocket next to a school radiator they would weld together forming a jewel-like cluster stuck to the paper bag. Breaking chunks off this gem would keep you occupied on long walks home.

The legacy of this youthful indulgence is some seriously expensive restorative dental work. If only I had known then what I know now, I would have married a dentist.

Intensely chocolaty with a seriously sticky coating, chocolate cracknel really gave the jaw muscles a workout. Luckily the brace wearers in the seventies were few and far between as eating this would put you back in the orthodontist's chair for an adjustment quicker than scoffing a roll of Toffos.

🖊 *Ingredients*

200g golden syrup
75g dried milk powder
75g puffed wheat
25g cocoa
120g butter or margarine

How to...

1. Melt the butter or margarine and syrup together in a large pan. Remove from the heat.
2. Sieve together the cocoa and dried milk powder.
3. Whisk the milk and cocoa into the saucepan containing the butter and syrup.
4. Once mixed thoroughly return to the heat and cook gently for 20 minutes, stirring often to prevent the mixture from catching on the bottom of the pan.
5. Remove the chocolate sauce from the heat and allow to cool slightly.
6. Place the puffed wheat in a large bowl and add the chocolate coating. Stir until all the puffed wheat is sticky and chocolaty. Press into a tin, cut into squares and leave to set.
7. Serve with pink or green custard as your mood dictates.

Chocolate biscuit cake

School radiators were huge. Big enough to rest a whole crate of milk bottles on defrosting gently until playtime. Large enough to find them draped with socks of every hue and aroma after a wet journey into school. There were scare stories too: sitting on them when warm brought dire warnings of chilblains. Taking a rest on a cold radiator came with horror stories about piles. Running a pencil along the radiator was tuneful and fun, but trying this with your finger could lead to a visit from the fire brigade as they attempted to extricate your digit. This would of course be after some wag had said, 'Oh, I have seen this before; they had to cut the finger off!' Not what a five-year-old wants to hear.

You knew the cold weather was here for a while if chocolate biscuit cake was on the menu. Some puddings were made to give us that additional warmth we needed in the wintertime. Chocolate biscuit cake was the complete opposite; it needed the cold winter weather to survive. It was held together by the action of the coldness on the butter and chocolate. As soon as the temperature climbed high enough to prevent your breath turning to steam as you walked to school this biscuit crumbled and fell into a pile of chocolate rubble.

✐ Ingredients

250g shortcake biscuits (cheap it says on
the recipe I was given!)

125g butter or margarine (melted)

1 tbsp cocoa

1 tbsp golden syrup

1 big bar chocolate, milk or plain as you prefer

How to...

1. In a mixing bowl, using the end of a rolling pin, crush the biscuits into crumbs. You could use the fill-a-plastic-bag-and-whack-with-a wooden-spoon method if you want. You could use a food processor, but that takes all the fun out of it.

2. In a large saucepan melt the butter, cocoa and syrup together to make a sauce.

3. Pour the chocolate sauce on to the biscuit crumbs and combine thoroughly.

4. Tip the chocolaty rubble into a buttered round sandwich tin and press down. Put into the fridge to set.

5. Once set melt the chocolate and pour over the biscuit base. Refrigerate once more until the chocolate is set. Cut into wedges and serve. This is best served from the fridge as it is only the cold that holds it together.

☀ Variations

The sheer chocolateness of this cries out for the addition of some fruit. I like to add snipped-up dried apricots into the biscuit base. Add in whatever you fancy. School cooks would have used glacé cherries. If you are going to please respect their values and buy the coloured ones!

Chocolate cornflake cake

The end of term was a peculiar time. Periods of manic rushing around and getting things finished were followed very quickly with vast spaces of time with little to do. Drawers were tidied, wall displays cleared and the lost property box was wheeled out to the front of school for mums to search through.

End of term performances and assemblies raised the profile of the chosen few. The rest of us sat in a pair of tights and a matching T-shirt pretending it was our choice to be a sheep in the Nativity play. Bringing in games for the last day was fun, except if you brought in Mousetrap: by the time you had finally got it set up, the bell went for home time.

These cakes were a real end of term treat. I can't think of another school meal where the cook made individual portions of anything. The queue was full of anxiety about getting the smallest cake, or heaven forbid, the one without the Smartie. We had these with a glass of orange juice or milky coffee. Very grown up we felt too.

✎ Ingredients

125g caster sugar
125g butter
220g cornflakes
25g cocoa
125g golden syrup

How to...

1. Line a patty tin with cake cases.
2. Place the sugar, syrup, cocoa and butter in a large pan and heat gently until the butter has melted. Give the mixture a good stir and add in the cornflakes a few handfuls at a time until either the cornflakes are all added or the chocolate mixture is all used up. Mix well to make sure each cornflake is sticky.
3. Spoon the cornflake mix into the cake cases. Fill each case generously and press down a little to ensure the cornflakes stick together.
4. Decorate each cornflake cake with a Smartie.
5. Refrigerate until the cakes have cooled and become hard.
6. Fight with your best friend for the last cake with an orange Smartie.

Coconut crisps

Keeping your mouth shut was always a problem. In class you were expected to stay quite unless answering a question. Very rarely did you get into groups to discuss anything. You thought twice about asking to borrow your friend's pencil in case you were accused of disrupting the lesson. On the rare occasions that you did have a sneaky chat you would invariably get caught. Just as you whispered some vital and very private piece of news to your friend the teacher would say, 'Would you like to share that with the rest of the class?' Almost certainly the answer would be 'No'.

Coconut crisps were not so much crisp as dense and chewy. These sticky treats were served with tangy yogurt or stewed fruit. They were presented as wedges so big it made it almost impossible to open your mouth wide enough to pass on any juicy pieces of gossip. Somehow or other I always managed it.

Ingredients

200g golden syrup

100g powdered milk

25g desiccated coconut

100g butter or margarine

200g Rice Krispies

How to...

1. In a large pan melt the butter or margarine and the syrup together.
2. Add the sieved dried milk and coconut and stir well.
3. Bring up to simmering point and barely simmer for 10 minutes or until the mixture turns to a darker golden brown. Keep stirring all the time.
4. Allow to cool for a few minutes.
5. Place the Rice Krispies in a large bowl and add the slightly cooled coconut mixture. Stir well.
6. Press into a baking tray about 12 inches by 7 inches and mark out bars.
7. Cool and cut following bar markings.

Oaty crunch

We sang some fantastic songs at my school. Our assembly songs were the usual standards of 'When a knight won his spurs', 'There was a green hill far away' and, if the pianist was up to it, 'Morning has broken'. The latter was always played with the twiddly bits, but not quite as written in the score I suspect. The plastic cover of our brightly coloured hymn book smelt of vanilla and we spent most of our assemblies covering our faces with the books. The teachers thought we were deep in contemplation but the truth is we were just breathing in that lovely smell.

In our singing lessons, we never called it music; we sang all manner of songs from 'Football crazy' to 'Daniel man jazz'. One very bizarre song we sang was all about the sinking of the Titanic. It had a really bouncy tune and we always requested it if we were given the choice. We didn't pay much attention to the words. Quite why anyone thought the lines 'Husbands and wives, little children lost their lives' sung to a cheery skipping tune was appropriate for nine-year-olds is beyond me. Still, we sang until our faces ached.

Sometimes singing was made harder than it should have been. I am sure the cook colluded with the teachers because after eating oaty crunch your jaw muscles needed a rest. 'Shall we get the chime bars out children?'

✐ Ingredients

225g plain flour
125g butter or margarine (at room temperature)
125g lard or white vegetable shortening
175g caster sugar
75g oats
75g desiccated coconut
1 tsp baking powder

How to...

1. Preheat oven to 170°C/Gas 4.

2. In a large bowl cream the sugar, shortening or lard and butter together. Beat until the colour changes to a very pale cream.

3. Sieve in the flour and baking powder and mix well. Add in the oats and coconut. Stir until well combined.

4. Grease a baking tray. Using a wet hand take walnut-sized pieces of biscuit mix and roll into a ball. Place on to baking trays and flatten slightly.

5. Bake for 10 minutes. Remove from trays and place on cooling racks.

6. Serve with cold custard decorated with hundreds and thousands.

Just as important to our enjoyment of any school dinner or pudding were the bits and pieces that accompanied the dish.

Poured, ladled or just dolloped, custards and sweet sauces transformed many very simple biscuits or cakes into a proper pudding. They softened the hard and sweetened the plain and on rare occasions, disguised the almost inedible. Very few puddings couldn't be enhanced by a slosh of chocolate sauce. A number of these sauces came only from school kitchens, pink custard and mint sauce being top of that list. They have achieved almost legendary status and a real cult following.

Many more mundane but vital pieces of the school-dinner jigsaw are included here. Please don't think I am patronising anyone by giving a recipe for mash or gravy; there is a method to making the perfect mash or gravy and sadly some of us were the recipients of the less than perfect varieties when we were at school. Follow these recipes and you shouldn't get the lumps.

Salads and suet pastry gave our dinners seasonality and the dumplings and short crust soaked up the gravy. Milky coffee kept us going until home time and white sauce could be flavoured to make even the blandest of foods tasty. As for the cobblers, they made us smirk and filled us up. We left the dinner hall happy and contented – what better recipe could there be?

* * *

These recipes make enough to supply that little extra for one family meal for four.

Extras

Custard

Custard divided us into three camps at school. Non-custard takers, although few and far between, did sadly exist. (Reader, I married him!) The other two camps were skin or not skin. I would fight tooth and nail to get to the front of the queue because I loved the variety of textures that the skin gave to my pudding. Watching the skin on the custard ripple, bulge and finally tumble out of the aluminium jug into my bowl was a joy. Skin haters slunk to the back of the queue and then panicked if the skin was still attached to the ladle as their scoop was served. Acting as a protective layer, it kept the heat in your pudding and glow in your cheeks.

School custard was always bright yellow, sweet and made with custard powder. Its purpose was to help get milk into the children in the post-war era. The fact that it softened the pastry and could help make a pudding go further was a bonus. Any leftovers were served with hundreds and thousands the following day – wonderful!

Please feel free to make the custard powder version, buy the instant packets or even a carton of ready-made if you so wish. I won't tell on you. However, real egg custard is great too and here is the recipe for that.

✎ Ingredients

300ml full cream milk (save the cream on the top
before you measure the milk out)

1 tbsp cream or top of the milk

Vanilla pod or vanilla extract

2 egg yolks (you can make meringues with the whites!)

1 tbsp caster sugar

How to...

1. Warm the milk and cream together but do not allow this to get too hot.
2. Whisk together the egg yolks, sugar and vanilla extract. If you are using a vanilla pod, split the pod, scrape out the seeds and whisk these into the egg and sugar mixture.
3. Pour the warm milk mixture over the eggs and sugar, whisking all the time until well combined.
4. Return to the saucepan and slowly bring to a simmer. With a wooden spoon keep stirring until the mixture thickens. Do not rush this or you will end up with sweetened scrambled eggs.
5. Pour over puddings, pies, stewed fruits or tarts and enjoy.

✳ Variations

If you are going to make custard often you might find that making vanilla sugar is more economical than buying lots of vanilla pods. Take a large screw-topped jar, pop in a vanilla pod and add in caster sugar to cover. Place the lid on the jar and leave for a week. The vanilla flavour will infuse with the sugar. Refill the jar as you go and you will have lovely vanilla-flavoured sugar for custards and cakes.

Mint custard

Green food wasn't that popular in school. This probably stemmed from the fact that green vegetables were often nuked to the point of disintegration in the sixties and seventies, green fruit was often very sharp and green breads and pastry were just plain mouldy.

The nanny state had yet to legislate on sell by or best before dates, so it was a time when it was up to you to decide if food was edible or not. Visiting the home of an elderly relative and accepting a bite to eat was like playing Russian roulette with your digestive system. Having lived through the war they were loath to throw anything away. Leftovers festered in the fridge, safe between two plates, until needed later in the week or month. Or even year.

This green food, however, never had the chance to make the leftovers bowl. Silken and smooth it coated all manner of chocolate puddings. Softening the chocolate concrete, puddled around the chocolate sponge or melting the sticky toffee of the chocolate cracknel, it enhanced the experience. Scraping the green away from the chocolate underneath wasn't to get rid of the nasty bits but merely a chance to save the best part till last.

🖉 Ingredients

300ml milk
20g cornflour
1 tbsp caster sugar
Peppermint extract
Green food colouring (optional)

How to...

1. Measure 300ml of milk into a jug.
2. In a small bowl mix together the sugar and cornflour and add several tablespoons of the milk to make a smooth paste.
3. Place the milk in a pan and add in the corn flour and sugar paste. Stir well to combine and slowly bring to the boil, stirring all the time.
4. As the mixture thickens add the peppermint extract to taste. If using the food colouring add now and serve with the chocolate pudding of your choice.

Pink custard

Rumours are what kept the children talking in the playground. Actually they kept the staff talking too, but usually those rumours often concerned much baser facts. I think I have already mentioned squirrel and kangaroo meat being used for the meat pies. Other 'facts' were that cauliflower was really brains and that anything green and mushy had to be made from snot or bogeys. So many rumours in fact that every playground had their own version of the following rhyme:

> Scab and puss custard,
> Snot and bogey pie,
> All mixed up with a dead dog's eye
> Stir it up, mash it up, eat it up quick,
> All washed down with a cup of cold sick

The stuff of more glorious legends as far as the school meal was concerned was pink custard. Lurid in colour, luscious in texture and loved almost universally, pink custard made a simple iced sponge into a proper pudding. In researching this recipe some have spoken of alchemy and others of food colouring and strawberry flavouring, but I have discovered the truth (I think). As with most truths it is very simple and uncomplicated and I will share it with you. Pink custard is just unset warm blancmange.

🖉 Ingredients
1 pint milk, plus a little extra if needed
1 packet pink blancmange mix
(strawberry and raspberry both work equally well)
2 or 3 tbs sugar to taste

How to...

1. In a heat-proof bowl empty the contents of a blancmange packet. Add the sugar and two or three tablespoons from the pint of milk and mix to a paste.
2. Heat the remaining milk in a pan until warm but not boiling. Pour a little of this milk on to the paste and give it a really good mix.
3. Pour this bright pink goo into the warmed milk and then bring to the boil. Keep stirring as it has a tendency to catch and burn if your mind wanders for a second. Simmer for about a minute. If the custard is very thick add a little more milk to thin it down. It should be poured over the sponge and not sliced!
4. Serve with iced vanilla sponge or chocolate sponge.
5. Any leftovers can be kept and served cold the next day. N.B. This is a rare event!

Mock cream

Milk monitor was a sought after position of power. Not only did you get to poke the straws through each individual bottle top, you also got to swan about the empty school corridors carrying the crates of milk from class to class.

Allowing pairs of small children to carry heavy crates of full glass bottles up and down polished marble-effect staircases and along shiny terrazzo corridors was a daily occurrence in all schools. Yet no one came to any serious harm. The paper straw may have bent on occasions and on wet days the water that gathered in the crate edges tipped on to your sock and down under the T-bar of your sandal, but nothing life threatening.

On days when the weather was icy and the milk was frozen the school smell of cauliflower, tobacco smoke and sweaty plimsoll was joined by the waft of curdling milk. Placing the crates near the radiators defrosted the milk brilliantly and gave the drinkers a choice of milk temperature. The advent of the tetrapak and plastic straws signalled the end of power for the milk monitor. Good grief, they even supply fridges for the milk now too.

Despite the free school milk we always had fake cream. Ah, where would a school tart be without a swirl of mock cream to adorn an otherwise naked top? Loved and hated in turns, mock cream would be licked off with gusto or saved till last. If you were lucky you might get someone else's too!

Ingredients

5g plain flour
100ml milk
50g caster sugar
70g butter
Vanilla extract

How to...

1. Mix the flour and a splash of the milk to a paste. Add the rest of the milk to this paste and put into a small saucepan. Heat gently, stirring constantly until the mix boils. Bring to a simmer; keep stirring for a further 3 minutes. Leave to one side to cool.

2. Cream together the butter and sugar. This is best done with an electric hand mixer as you need to cream the butter and sugar until it is no longer grainy and has become very pale.

3. Check the flour and milk mix has cooled.

4. When cooled use the electric hand mixer again to combine the creamed butter and sugar mixture with the flour and milk mix. Add the vanilla extract at this point. Beat together until the mock cream is light and airy. This may take a moment or two.

5. Pipe on to jam tart, chocolate tart or even jelly.

Chocolate custard

Every school had different rituals at lunchtime. In my primary school grace was said, but the logistics of getting everyone into the canteen and served meant we didn't actually say grace until the last person had been served. Sometimes you were on to your pudding when the bell rang for grace to be said:

> *Ding ding ding*
> *Stand up.*
> *Hands together and eyes closed everybody.*
> *'Thank you for the world so sweet, Thank you for the*
> *food we eat, Thank you for the birds that sing,*
> *Thank you God for everything. Amen.'*

On most occasions this was little more than an inconvenience, but on chocolate sponge and custard days having to stop midway probably began my life of doubt and questioning. I never closed my eyes just in case anyone took the chance to have a sly spoonful of my pudding. I would rather have incurred the wrath of God than let some little toad swipe my chocolate custard.

This is absolutely not to be confused with chocolate sauce. Chocolate custard is made with milk and has the ability to form a rather, in my case, sought after skin. Often served with chocolate sponge or tinned mandarins it was, and still is, glorious.

🍫 *Ingredients*

300ml milk
20g cornflour
1 tbsp cocoa
1 tbsp caster sugar

How to...

1. Measure 300ml of milk into a jug.
2. In a small bowl mix together the sugar, cocoa and cornflour and add several tablespoons of the milk to make a smooth paste.
3. Place the milk in a pan and add in the chocolate paste. Stir well to combine and slowly bring to the boil, stirring all the time.
4. As the mixture thickens keep stirring. If no one else has noticed that you have made this slink quietly into a corner and enjoy with chocolate sponge pudding without having to share with anyone.

Gravy

Oranges and browns were big in the seventies. Brown carpets, orange upholstery, brown and orange chunky tableware; we even had chocolate-brown velvet curtains! The walls of my parent's small suburban hallway were decorated with orange circles the size of large dinner plates. Standing and looking at these for too long could bring about a psychedelic experience without resorting to chemicals of any kind.

Britain seemed covered in a wave of browns and oranges with the occasional hint of beige. These colours could be dark and dismal, depressing even, but the one brown thing that always made my heart soar was gravy.

A deep chestnut liquid that could transform the chewiest pastry or the blandest vegetables into seasoned offerings, school gravy was wonderful.

The majority of these gravies were made with care and lashings of gravy browning or powder. I doubt very much that pans were scraped of their Marmite-like meat juices and cooked out in a roux with red wine and stock. Proper gravy is what I'm giving you the recipe for but occasionally we all need to resort to the instant sort and that is nothing to be ashamed of either.

✐ Ingredients

Roasting dish containing cooking residues

1 tbsp plain flour

500ml warm stock (choose one that matches
the roast you are cooking)

1 glass wine

How to...

1. When you roast your joint of meat put some vegetables and woody herbs under it to act both as a trivet to keep the meat out of the fat and also to provide additional flavour for your gravy. I use onions and carrots under beef, onions, unpeeled garlic and lemon wedges under chicken. For pork I use onions, apple slices and sage leaves. Lamb joints are placed on lemon wedges, unpeeled garlic and rosemary.

2. Tip the pan and drain the fat and juices to one corner of the pan. Remove the majority of the fat. I aim to leave about one to two tablespoons of fat in the pan.

3. Place the roasting tin on a very low heat on the hob and tip in the flour. Using a wooden spoon or a whisk cook the fat and flour together to create a paste. As you do, scrape all the tasty dark bits up from the bottom of the pan.

4. After a minute of cooking out the floury taste add a glass of wine (whatever you are drinking with the meal) to the tray and allow to bubble. Now add the warm stock a little at a time until all incorporated. You may not need it all; stop when the gravy is the thickness your family likes. If the gravy looks too thin don't panic there is a solution.

5. Pass the gravy through a sieve to remove the vegetable bits and any lumps. If it looks too thin return to a pan and reduce down until the gravy has thickened. Taste and season with salt and pepper.

6. Stir in any additional flavours such as mustard for beef or redcurrant jelly for lamb.

7. Pour over anything and everything.

Mashed potato

Memories of mashed potato at school can be summed up in one word: lumps. These were partly caused by ineffective cooking and mashing. But the type of potato chosen for cooking made a difference too. School cooks bought their spuds by the half-hundred weight. In the days before traceability, named heritage varieties and labelling bags with the farmer's inside leg measurements, the choice was reds or whites.

We have much more choice now so lumpy mash should be a thing of the past. You need to choose a floury potato with fairly high starch content. Don't even think about mashing a waxy potato. As well as the right potato you need a sturdy masher or potato ricer to bash the lumps out. I wouldn't use a mixer as it makes the mash too sticky for my liking. If you want to continue the school-dinner mash experience to its bitter end then you will also need to purchase a scoop. The heavy duty ratchet types were the ones chosen by dinner ladies, and who am I to contradict the professionals?

Ingredients

1 kg potatoes
100ml warm milk
Several knobs of butter
Salt and pepper

How to...

1. Peel and cube potatoes. Place in a large saucepan and cover with cold salted water. Bring to the boil and simmer for 10 to 15 minutes until cooked through but not disintegrating.

2. Drain in a colander and return to the pan. Place the pan over a very low heat for a minute or so to drive off any excess moisture.

3. Mash or rice the potatoes well, adding in the milk as you go. The milk must be warm or the starches in the potato will become gluey and the mash will cool down.

4. Add in as much butter as you like, beating with a wooden spoon. Taste and season.

5. Scoop on to a plate and serve with any meal you like. If you can't be bothered cooking anything else just stir in a large handful of grated cheese, put on a movie and have a quiet night in.

☀ Variations

These are endless but can include olive oil instead of butter, olives or tapenade, pesto, soured cream and chives, spring onions, fried onions, wholegrain mustard, garlic, sweet potato and carrots. Go on, be adventurous.

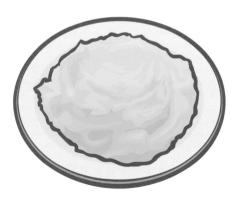

Shortcrust pastry

From county to county, and from local authority to local authority, school dinners had many elements in common. Water was poured from large, often dented, metal jugs into our individual pastel-coloured metallic cups. Ladles dispensed anything liquid, from stew to custard, often from a great height. Large rectangular trays with lids held all our baked meals and puddings cut neatly into squares for serving.

Every meal had some form of pastry. Designed originally to prevent the filling from making a serious mess on the bottom of ovens, pastry has evolved into an integral part of the meal. Creating the ultimate tart's bottom or pie top was a way to fill us even fuller. It helped with portion control and those pie tops kept the heat in too. School pastry, it should be noted, was only ever savoury, never sweet. There wasn't time to make two pastry batches and, anyway, the pudding fillings were so sweet that the savoury pastry added a little something to the dish.

🖉 Ingredients

250g plain flour

125g butter, margarine, vegetable shortening or even lard
(or a combination of any of these), fridge cold

Cold water

How to...

① Preheat oven to 200°C/Gas 6.

② Cold hands make the best pastry so don't even contemplate this with sweaty palms! Wash your hands in cold water and make sure you work in the coolest part of your kitchen.

③ Place flour and fat into a large bowl and rub in the fat using just your fingertips until the mixture resembles breadcrumbs. Using a round-bladed knife stir in the cold water a little at a time until the mixture begins to come together. Use your hands to form a ball of pastry. Wrap the pastry in cling film and rest for half an hour or so in the fridge. (If this is too much trouble then buy the pastry – no one will ever know!)

④ Baking blind means baking empty except for a scrunched foil lining or foil and baking (not baked!) beans.

⑤ Roll out the pastry, line a tin 14 inches by 8 inches. Prick with a fork, fill with baking beans and bake blind for 15 minutes. Allow to cool.

Dumplings

If you were lucky and the teacher had a good aim the chalk would whistle past your ear. This gentle reminder to pay attention worked very well with few of us risking misbehaviour. If the chalk failed, the big guns came out in the form of the board rubber. This was never thrown to hit but some of the older male teachers could get it to whistle past your head within the width of a gnat's eyelash. Failure to get the trajectory right led to loss of teeth or concussion. It would, however, have been your fault for moving your head at the last moment.

On bad dumpling days I often wondered if the same teachers wouldn't use the more leaden dumplings to reprimand the noisier elements in the dinner hall. Dumplings are the culinary equivalent of a sponge, sucking up the tastiest juices from the casserole or soup. If you were lucky they were as light as a feather and filled your tummy with a gentle warming glow. If you weren't lucky they would resemble a shot putt landing in your guts for the rest of the day.

Ingredients

250g plain flour

125g suet

2 tsp baking powder

A good pinch of salt

3 or 4 tbs cold water

How to...

1 Stir together the flour, baking powder and suet using a round-ended knife. Try to touch the pastry as little as possible. Stir in the water little by little until the pastry forms a ball of dough. Lightly use your hands to bring the final ball together.

2 Pinch off walnut-sized balls of dough and gently roll them in your hands to make them more or less spherical.

3 Lower these into the cooking pot and place on the lid. Do not open the lid for the next 25 minutes unless you are fond of cannonball-type dumplings.

4 Warm a bowl and serve yourself a large ladleful of casserole and dumplings.

☀ Variation

The suet crust topping a steak and kidney pie was really just one enormous dumpling.

1 *Make the pastry as above and then pat out until large enough to fit the casserole.*

2 *Remove the casserole from the oven, place the pie crust on top of the steak and kidney, pressing down to make sure it is in contact with the meat, and replace the casserole lid.*

3 *Bake for an hour and a half. Don't peek, you will deflate the crust. Lift the lid, breathe in the smells and reluctantly call the rest of the diners to share the meal.*

Cobbler topping

As soon as we got a letter telling us we would be on a coach for a school trip we began to plan the songs we were going to sing. 'Ten green bottles' was one favourite. 'She'll be coming round the mountain' was another. 'They took the flying fortress up forty thousand feet' gave us immense pleasure recalling the horrific death of a parachutist to the tune of 'Glory, glory, hallelujah'. Some songs were just downright mind bending, no more so than 'I know a song that will get on your nerves'. Usually we managed about 15 minutes before we were told that our singing was distracting the driver and we needed to stop.

Seeing cobblers on the menu gave everyone the excuse to say a slightly naughty word over and over again until told to stop. I feel certain that we were told to be quiet not because the word was that rude but mainly as we were getting silly and extremely irritating. These dense and chewy little rounds aided portion control I have no doubt, but the cobbler's glossy exterior and cheesy crunch was pure heaven.

✏ Ingredients

175g self-raising flour
30g butter or margarine
125g strong cheddar cheese, grated
1 egg, beaten
1 tbs milk

How to...

1. Place all the dry ingredients into a roomy bowl. Rub the butter or margarine into the flour until the mix resembles breadcrumbs. Stir in the grated cheese.

2. Use a round-ended knife and mix in the egg and enough milk to make the dough come together. Use your hands to pat out the dough until about 2cm thick and cut out rounds using a pastry cutter. The secret is to be gentle with the dough.

3. Place these rounds on to your chosen casserole and brush with a little beaten egg or milk.

4. Return the casserole to the oven and bake for a further 25 to 30 minutes until golden brown.

5. Adding a little dry mustard to the flour will give the cobblers a little kick, as will any herbs. Add whatever you think will complement the casserole they accompany. Horseradish or mustard would be great with a beef casserole and lemon thyme would be fabulous with chicken.

White sauce

Hiding the truth and making up stories to back up arguments is something in which adults have colluded since time began. Children quickly recognise the sound of the bell on the ice cream van but if they have been told it only plays that tune when it has run out of ice cream they hopefully won't keep pestering you for a 99 with nuts and sauce just when you are ready to dish up tea.

Often it has been vital to camouflage food that children were not too keen on too, and white sauce is incredibly versatile in this respect. So often seen as the base of cheese sauce, it can be enriched with an egg yolk, pepped up with a little mustard powder and made glossy with an extra knob of butter at the end. The way white sauce coats the mouth is the secret of its success. If you don't do dairy you can use warm stock in place of the milk. Make your sauce with a whisk and plenty of energy and you should not have too many problems with lumps. Best of all, get a fellow diner to do the whisking and then if the white sauce is lumpy it won't be your fault.

✏️ *Ingredients*

25g flour
25g butter
½ to ¾ pt milk
Salt and white pepper

How to...

1. Melt the butter over a low heat in a large pan, add the flour and, whisking gently, cook out for a minute. This will prevent your sauce from tasting too floury. Add the milk and whisk in to prevent lumps. I use a balloon whisk but use what you feel works for you.

2. Cook until the sauce thickens. Once at the thickness you need for your dish cook about 30 seconds more. You may need to add less than the milk quantity shown here. Season to taste. White pepper is used so you don't get black flecks and accusations that you burnt the sauce from those critics at your table.

3. Add in cheese now for a cheese sauce, sautéed mushrooms for a mushroom sauce, grain mustard for mustard sauce or parsley for a fish pie sauce.

4. Pour over whatever needs hiding and feign surprise when the offending food stuff is discovered.

Milky coffee

Imagine our feelings of sophistication then when milky coffee and buns were listed as a pudding on the school-dinner menu. If you suggested giving children caffeine at school now questions would be asked in Parliament. Taking our cue from the adults we put the world to rights over the tightly held mugs. Only the fact that it was served from a large urn reminded us that we were only 12 and sitting in the school canteen and not a Soho coffee house as we imagined.

Coffee, if you had it at home, was a bit of a performance. The instant varieties tasted insipid so out would come one of a variety of coffee machines. Now we aren't talking the shiny steam-belching espresso-making machines that were found on an Italian restaurant's bar. No, we had percolators that plopped away in the background or very fragile glass globes that fitted together over a spirit lamp at the end of dinner parties. Too many glasses of Liebfraumilch and the coffee machines were harder to put together than an Airfix kit. Mellow Birds anyone?

🖉 Ingredients

Coffee (real or instant, you choose)

Warm milk

Sugar (if required)

Philosophical argument to debate

How to...

1. Warm the milk until just below boiling point.
2. Mix milk and the made up coffee in equal quantities.
3. Sweeten to taste. Brown sugar was much more grown up than white we found.
4. Take a slice of Swedish tea ring or a piece of flapjack to your table.
5. Put the world to rights or discuss your history homework, whichever is the most pressing.

Winter salad

Rabbit food, as a salad was often described, had a very bad press. This was partly because many people were suspicious of meals that didn't contain meat and two veg. It was also because salad in the seventies usually meant a couple of lettuce leaves, a few rings of cucumber, half a tomato, some cress and possibly a scattering of beetroot cubes. A dollop of salad cream on the side and that was it. This was always accompanied by a slice or two of cold meat. Usually ham or beef, but at an elderly relative's you might get pressed tongue if you were very unfortunate.

There was, however, a winter salad too. Served to us at school, we had fewer of the prejudices of the older generation, so it was a real favourite. The sweetness of the ingredients appealed to our taste buds too. Using carrots as the main bulk of the salad, it was a little like coleslaw without the mayonnaise, though I do remember peanuts being another occasional part of this dish (obviously before we were aware people could be allergic to them!). Sometimes grated apple went in as well as the raisins. I don't recall any oil or dressing being used but lemon juice or possibly vinegar gave winter salad a lift as it was probably very sweet without it.

✐ Ingredients

450g carrots, peeled and finely grated

100g sultanas or raisins

25g chopped salted peanuts

1 green apple, grated

Squeeze of lemon or splash of vinegar

Salt and pepper

How to...

1. Peel and grate the carrots finely. Grate but don't peel the apple. If the grated apple is very juicy drain a little of the juice before mixing with the carrot.

2. Stir in the peanuts and raisins and add a splash of lemon or vinegar if you need to.

3. Season to taste and leave for 10 minutes for the flavours to combine and the raisins to soften a little.

Index